YOUNG VIC

The Misanthrope
Molière

Version by Martin Crimp

faber and faber
LONDON · BOSTON

FUNDED BY
LONDON BOROUGHS GRANTS COMMITTEE

LAMBETH
ENVIRONMENTAL SERVICES

LONDON
ARTS BOARD

BOX OFFICE COMPUTERISED BY
DIGITAL EQUIPMENT CO. LIMITED digital

First published in 1996
by Faber and Faber Limited
3 Queen Square London WC1N 3AU

Printed in England by Clays Ltd, St Ives plc

A CIP record for this book
is available from the British Library

ISBN 0–571–17909–6

2 4 6 8 10 9 7 5 3 1

THE YOUNG VIC THEATRE

In 1968 Lord Olivier and the National Theatre (then based at the Old Vic) talked of a theatre which would form a centre of work particularly accessible to students and young people. The theatre's programme was to include the classics, new plays, experimental theatre and educational work.

The Young Vic was established in September 1970 by Frank Dunlop and became the first major theatre producing work for younger audiences. In 1974 the Young Vic became independent of the National and went on to establish an international reputation for its productions, developing a wide-ranging audience of all ages and backgrounds.

During 1995-96 the theatre celebrates its 25th anniversary, having created an enormous range and style of work, from Beckett to Sophocles and Shakespeare to Lennon, including the world premiere of **Joseph and the Amazing Technicolor Dreamcoat** (Tim Rice and Andrew Lloyd Webber), Arthur Miller's **The Last Yankee** and the British premiere of Tom Stoppard's **Rosencrantz and Guildenstern are Dead**. More recent highly successful Young Vic productions include Tim Supple's critically acclaimed **The Slab Boys Trilogy** written by John Byrne, a stage adaptation of four stories from Kipling's **The Jungle Book** and the smash hit **Grimm Tales** for which Tim was awarded **Best Director - Off West End** by London's Time Out Magazine.

The Young Vic continues its commitment to creating adventurous theatre for as wide an audience as possible and particularly the young. As London's only theatre-in-the-round and most adaptable thrust stage, the Young Vic offers unique opportunities for the exploration of intimate ensemble performance and the imaginative use of space, light and sound.

'Both the building and the stage/audience relationship are unique and altogether vital to the theatre scene of the metropolis'.

Trevor Nunn

RE-WRITING MOLIÈRE

For all its formal brilliance, **le Misanthrope** (1666) is one of Molière's most intensely personal plays. The fierce argument between conformity and non-conformity clearly derives from his experience of the scandals surrounding three plays of the early 1660's - **l'Ecole des Femmes**, **le Tartuffe** and **Dom Juan** - where the writer found himself accused of obscenity, and, more dangerously, of atheism. The voices of righteous anger (Alceste) on the one hand, and reasonable compromise (Philinte) on the other, must have been continually whispering inside his head like good and bad angels as he struggled to come to terms with the ambiguity of his position as both satirist and servant of the cultural and political elite. It's hard not to see in the play's central relationship - etched in acid - between a middle-aged man and a woman half his age a reference to Molière's own personal life, after his marriage in 1662, aged 40, to Armande Béjart, a young actress of 'vingt ans ou environ'. Equally, it would be a mistake to see Alceste as a self-portrait. The writer remains detached from his character. This is why Alceste, despite the serious overtones, remains a comic creation. In the words of Francine Mallet, 'Alceste is Molière without the irony. Molière knows he looks ridiculous in some situations - Alceste doesn't.'

So how do you 'translate' (literally 'move from one place to another') an artefact that is so much a product of 17th century Paris and Versailles? One answer - and the one I've attempted here - is to opt for a contemporary setting, and then explore the consequences - whatever deviations and departures from the original that may involve. Molière himself was adamant about the actuality of comedy: 'When you portray [tragic] heroes, you can do what you like. They're imaginary portraits, in which we don't expect to recognise ourselves... But when you portray real people, you have to paint what you see. The pictures must be accurate. If you don't make *recognisable portraits of the contemporary world*, then nothing's been achieved.' (La Critique de l'Ecole des Femmes, scene vi, italics mine.) And if, 300 years later, reflecting the contemporary world has meant taking certain 'liberties' with the text, this is only in the belief that - at this distance in time - re-invention, re-writing of one writer's work by another is 'fidelity' of the truest and most passionate kind.

On 17th February 1673, Molière, whose health had been deteriorating for some time, coughed up blood during the final scene of **le Malade Imaginaire**, at the point where the character he played was being 'initiated' as a doctor, in a scathing parody of the medical profession he so abhorred. After the performance he was carried in his chair back to his home in the rue de Richelieu. Two priests refused to come, and a third was too late: he died the same night, aged 51.

His enemies weren't slow to savour the irony. One anonymous poem puts these words into his mouth:

> 'I performed character-assassinations
> with impunity on kings, the devout, marquis, people of all stations.
> I found the hidden truth behind every character,
> but came to grief playing the part of doctor.
> I died without medical, spiritual or legal aid.
> I played death itself - and with death itself I paid.'

A week after Molière's death, on 24th February, his theatre re-opened with a production of **le Misanthrope**.

For background to Molière's life and work I am indebted to Francine Mallet's MOLIERE (Grasset, Paris 1986) from which I have quoted above.

Martin Crimp, November 1995.

Molière

Molière was born Jean Poquelin in 1622, the son of a prosperous upholsterer of Paris. His father was attached to the service of the King and Molière was intended to succeed him, however, in 1643 he changed his surname and joined a family of actors, the Béjarts, in their efforts to establish a theatre group called l'Illustre-Théâtre. This enterprise failed in Paris and the group embarked on an extensive tour of the provinces in a repertory of old French comedies and extemporized farces in the style of the commedia dell'arte. Encouraged by their touring success the group returned to Paris and performed in front of Louis XIV and his Court. The success of Molière's farce **le Docteur Amoureux** (The Amorous Doctor) gave the group the opportunity to share a theatre at the Petit-Bourbon with an Italian company already established there and it was here that Molière's reputation was established.

By 1663 Molière's pre-eminence in Parisien theatre was virtually unchallenged and Louis XIV himself danced in several of his ballets. Molière's marriage in 1662, to the youngest Béjart daughter Armande, led to scandal as his close relationship with the family encouraged his enemies to declare that he had married his own daughter. The King, however, maintained his patronage and continued to do so throughout the uproar caused by many of his plays, amongst others, **Dom Juan** (1665), considered blasphemous and **le Tartuffe** (1665) a study of hypocrisy which infuriated the bigots of Paris. None of this endangered the success of such plays as **le Medecin Malgre Lui** (The Reluctant Doctor), **les Fourberies de Scapin** (Scapino's Tricks), **le Malade Imaginaire** (The Hypochondriac) and, of course, **le Misanthrope**.

Molière's influence on European theatre is of great significance. He raised comedy to the heights that had only previously been attained in tragedy and his great roles continue to demonstrate the excellence of successive generations of actors.

Martin Crimp

Work for theatre includes: **Dealing With Clair, Play With Repeats, No One Sees The Video, Getting Attention**, and **The Treatment**, winner of the 1993 John Whiting Award.

Forthcoming projects are a new play, **Attempts On Her Life**, and a translation of Koltès' **Roberto Zucco**, both for the Royal Court.

SUPPORT THE
YOUNG VIC
BECOME A **friend**

'The Young Vic is a unique part of our theatre heritage'
Dame Judi Dench

Join our Friends Scheme and your support will immediately help the Young Vic continue to create outstanding, innovative theatre. Becoming a friend also enables you to join more fully in the life of the theatre by taking advantage of these excellent benefits:

friend £20.00 annual subscription

- **Two half-price preview tickets to all Young Vic Company productions**
- **Regular advance information**
- **Priority booking**
- **Invitations to special Friends performances**

PLUS

- The **Young Vic Newsletter** featuring interviews with performers, directors and designers as well as inside information on Young Vic activities and events.

supporting friend £50.00 annual subscription

- **Six half-price preview tickets to all Young Vic Company productions**
- **Regular advance information**
- **Priority booking**
- **Reserved seating**
- **Invitations to special Friends performances**

PLUS

- The **Young Vic Newsletter** featuring interviews with performers, directors and designers as well as inside information on Young Vic activities and events.

junior friend £5.00 annual subscription

If you are under 16 years of age, become a Junior Friend for only £5.00 per year and receive:

- **Your own personal Young Vic card**
- **Regular advance information**
- **Invitations to Junior Friends performances**
- **The Young Vic Newsletter**

To find out more about the advantages of becoming a **Young Vic Friend** or to join the free mailing list contact Sophie Byatt on 0171 633 0133 or pick up a leaflet in the foyer.

A co-production with
the West Yorkshire Playhouse

Theatre de Complicite

based on the novel by **J M Coetzee**
adapted by **Mark Wheatley**

co-directed by Annie Castledine and Marcello Magni
design, projections and lighting by Peter Mumford
costume design by Idit Nathan

Being a True Account of a Year Spent on a Desert Island With
Many Strange Circumstances Never Hitherto Related

**"Complicite... a company of quite
exceptional originality"** Daily Telegraph

Young Vic
The Cut, London SE1 8LZ

24 April to 1 June
Box Office/cc 0171 928 6363

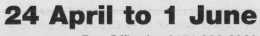

THE YOUNG VIC STUDIO THIS SPRING

WINK

'this is as fine a work of total theatre as one could hope to find....a joy to behold'
Time Out on Wink's production of **The Lizzie Play**.

31 January to 17 February	Wink present **The Art of Random Whistling**
Tickets £8.00	Text by Mark Jenkinson
Concessions £6.00	

> *A mother is typing, a couple laugh, someone swears, a girl is singing,*
> *the Spanish man plays his piano too loud. A child disappears.*

Continuing in Wink's ensemble style, **The Art of Random Whistling** is an atmospheric symphony of human interaction, integrating a vivid soundscape and strong visual language to recount a tale of collective experience; a celebration of humanity within contemporary city life. **Wink** are Natasha Chivers, Katrina Lindsay and Rufus Norris.

TALAWA THEATRE COMPANY

'Talawa are magnificent' The Independent

19 February to 30 March	Talawa Theatre Company present ZEBRA CROSSING, a
Tickets £8.00	season of Black performance at the Young Vic Studio.
Concessions £5.00	
Saturday matinees £6.00	
All preview tickets £5.00	

ZEBRA CROSSING - Talawa presents a diverse choice of performance, poetry, music, film, new work and exclusive masterclasses, set within an interactive environment designed by Sue Mayes, from the new wave of Black British creators and performers.

From You to Me to You by Dorothea Smartt and Sherlee Mitchell

A Dolls House by Henrik Ibsen

The Men I've Had by Amanda Symonds and Warren Wills

New Work Commissioned by Talawa

le soir avec roney-fm! by ronald fraser-munro

The Looking Glass by Kole Onile-Ere

To Rahtid by Sol B. River

MASTERCLASSES

Talawa offers a season of masterclasses, opening with internationally acclaimed Jamaican opera star **Willard White** and closing with celebrated Indian actress **Alaknander Samarth**. These maestros impart their inspiring skills in two exclusive classes only. Early booking is advised.

TALKING TEXTS - a women writers' seminar for Black and Asian women.

For further details concerning masterclasses and the seminar please call **Talawa** on **0171 251 6644**.

SCARLET THEATRE

'The bold sensitive Scarlet Theatre' The Times

2 April to 20 April	Scarlet Theatre present **The Fruit Has Turned to Jam In the Fields**
Tickets £8.00	Co-Directed by Emma Bernard and Gráinne Byrne
Concessions £6.00	Text and concept Jyll Bradley
	Designed by Belinda Ackermann

Come on a surreal journey through the world of TV sit-com nostalgia - and beyond. Where three war-zoned women, Captain Mandarin, Sergeant Winsome and Corporal Trout find themselves called upon to defend the home front with an explosive mix of heroism, romance and unlimited fruit scones.

To book tickets for all **Young Vic Studio** performances ring the Box Office on 0171 928 6363

The Misanthrope
Molière

Version by Martin Crimp

A Young Vic Company Production

CAST *in order of appearance*

    John William Osborne

    Alceste Ken Stott

    Covington Niall Buggy

    Jennifer Elizabeth McGovern

    Ellen Cathryn Bradshaw

    Alexander Richard O'Callaghan

    Julian Jo Stone-Fewings

    Messenger/Simon George Beach

    Marcia Linda Marlowe

Directed by Lindsay Posner
Designed by Joanna Parker
Lighting Designed by Simon Corder
Original Music by Paddy Cunneen
Sound Designed by John A. Leonard
Musician Andrea Hess
Assistant Director Blake Lawit

First performance February 8 1996 at the Young Vic Theatre
Press night February 13 1996

GEORGE BEACH - Simon/Messenger
Theatre includes: **The Father** (PW Productions). **A Brief Affair** (Adam House and Pentameters Theatre, Hampstead). **On the Side of the Angels** (Adam House). Television includes: **Inspector Morse** (Zenith Productions). **Seaforth**, **Harry** and **The Entertainer** (BBC). **Soldier, Soldier** (Central TV). **The Bill** (Thames TV). **Covington Cross** (ABC/Reeves Entertainment). **Berlin Break** (Oceanic Productions). **Poirot** (LWT). Composer and Musical Director for **Pinocchio** (Shaw Theatre), **The Nose** (Old Red Lion Theatre and Wimbledon Theatre) and **On the Side of the Angels** (Blue Harlequin Theatre Company).

CATHRYN BRADSHAW - Ellen
Theatre includes: **Mirandolina** (Bristol Old Vic), **Tess** (Salisbury Playhouse), **The Tutor** (The Old Vic), **Hamlet** (Cheek by Jowl), **Bourgeois Gentilhomme** (Royal National Theatre), **Assassins** (The Donmar Warehouse), **Search and Destroy**, **The Man of Mode** and **The Libertine** (Royal Court), **The Last Waltz** (Greenwich Theatre), **The Seagull** and **Adam Bede** (Orange Tree Theatre). Television includes: **Inspector Morse** (Zenith), **Oranges Are Not the Only Fruit**, **Casualty**, **A Skirt Through History** and **Black Daisies for the Bride** (BBC). **Chancer** and **Boon** (Central), **Poirot** (LWT), **Frank Stubbs II** (Noel Gay TV). Film: **Bert Rigby You're a Fool** (Lorimar). Radio includes: **Riding High**, **When We Are Married**, **The Country Wife** and **Sense and Sensibility** (BBC).

NIALL BUGGY - Covington
Theatre includes: **Dead Funny** (Hampstead and Vaudeville Theatre) for which he won an Olivier Award for Best Comedy Actor. **The Rivals**, **Rough Crossing**, **Love for Love**, **Threepenny Opera** (Royal National Theatre). **School for Scandal**, **Hamlet**, and **Arms and the Man** (Haymarket Theatre, Leicester). **The Birthday Party**, **Waiting for Godot**, and **Salad Days** (Crucible Theatre, Sheffield). **Juno and the Paycock** (Albery Theatre) for which he received a TMA Martini Award. **Aristocrats** (Hampstead Theatre and New York) for which he won a Time Out Award, OBIE and Drama Desk Award (New York) and was nominated for a Clarence Derwent Award. Television includes: **Full Wax**, **Once in a Lifetime**, and **The Hummingbird Tree** (BBC). **Father Ted Crilly** (Channel 4), **Little Napoleons** (Picture Palace). Film includes: **The Lonely Passion of Judith Hearne** (Handmade Films), **King David** (Paramount Pictures), **The Playboys** (directed by Gillies McKinnon), **Close My Eyes** (directed by Stephen Poliakoff).

ELIZABETH McGOVERN - Jennifer
Theatre includes: **A Midsummer Night's Dream**, **As You Like It**, **Map of the World** (N.Y Shakespeare Festival). **Hamlet** (Roundabout Theatre, New York). **The Three Sisters** (Atlantic Theatre Company, New York). **When I Was a Girl I Used to Scream and Shout** (South Coast Rep.). **Aunt Dan and Lemon** (Mark Taper Forum, L.A). Television includes: **The Changeling** (directed by Simon Curtis), **Tales from Hollywood** (directed by Howard Davies), **HBO Men and Women Series** (HBO). Films include: **Ordinary People** (directed by Robert Redford), **Once Upon a Time in America** (directed by Sergio Leone). **She's Having a Baby** (directed by John Hughes). **Wings of Courage** (directed by Jean Jacques Annaud). **King of the Hill** (directed by Steven Soderbergh). **Racing with the Moon** (directed by Richard Benjamin). **The Bedroom Window** (directed by Curtis Hanson). **The Handmaid's Tale** (directed by Volker Schlondorff), **Ragtime** (directed by Milos Forman) for which she was nominated for an Academy Award.

LINDA MARLOWE - Marcia
Theatre includes: **The Trial**, **Hamlet**, **Greek**, **Decadence** and **Metamorphosis** (directed by Steven Berkoff). **Oedipus**, **The Virtuoso** and **Twelfth Night** (Royal Shakespeare Company). **Too Clever by Half**, **A Flea in Her Ear** (The Old Vic). **Bremen Coffee** (The Traverse and Hampstead Theatre). **A Streetcar Named Desire** (Sherman Theatre). **One Small Step** (one woman show).
Linda was a founder member, co-writer and performer for **Sadista Sisters Rock Theatre Group**. Television includes: **Love Hurts**, **Metamorphosis**, **The Green Man** (BBC). **She's Out** by Lynda la Plante and **Class Act** (Cinema Verity). Radio includes: **Macbeth** (with Steven Berkoff). **Poonsh** (by Snoo Wilson). **Proust, The Screenplay** (by Harold Pinter). Film includes: **Beckett**, **Zapper's Blade of Vengeance** and **Mr Love**. Directing includes: **A View from the Bridge** and **A Madhouse in Goa** (Oldham Coliseum), **Through the Leaves** (Leicester Studio). **Invade My Privacy** (Riverside Studios).

RICHARD O'CALLAGHAN - Alex
Theatre includes: **Spring Awakening**, **Three Months Gone** and **Macbeth** (Royal Court Theatre). **Butley** (Criterion Theatre). **Amadeus** (Her Majesty's Theatre). **Twelfth Night**, **Measure for Measure**, **Hamlet**, **Love's Labours Lost**, **Ricochet** and **Comedy of Errors** (Royal Shakespeare Company). **Animal Farm**, **Secret Rapture**, **King Lear** and **Richard III** (Royal National Theatre). **A Midsummer Night's Dream** and **The Boys from Syracuse** (The Open Air Theatre, Regent's Park). Television includes: **Renoir My Father**, **The Merry Wives of Windsor** and **Professional Foul** (BBC). **Mr Pye** (Landseer Films). **Born and Bred** (Thames TV).

WILLIAM OSBORNE - John
Theatre includes: **Absolute Hell** and **La Grande Magia** (Royal National Theatre). **The Strip** (Royal Court Theatre). **The Rivals** (Chichester Festival Theatre and The Albery Theatre). **The Deep Blue Sea** (The Almeida Theatre). **The Case of the Frightened Lady** (The Palace Theatre, Watford). **The Secret Agent** (Etcetera

Theatre). **Screamers** (The Arts Theatre). Television includes: **Cold Comfort Farm** (Thames TV). **Fall from Grace** (Portman Productions). **Pie in the Sky** (SelecTV). **Look at It This Way** and **Victoria Wood** (BBC), **Young Indy** (Lucas Films). Film: **Tom and Viv** (directed by Brian Gilbert). **Damage** (directed by Louis Malle).

JO STONE-FEWINGS - Julian
Theatre includes: **The Park** and **Henry VI, Part III** (Royal Shakespeare Company). **Fuente Ovejuna** and **Ghetto** (Royal National Theatre). **One Over the Eight** (Scarborough Theatre). **The Importance of Being Earnest** (Manchester Royal Exchange tour). Television includes: **London's Burning** and **The Prince** (LWT). **Waiting for God, Moon and Son, Dodgem** and **Casualty** (BBC), **The Bill** (Thames TV). **Shrinks** (Euston), **Medics** (Granada), **Soldier, Soldier** (Central). Radio: **The Secret Life** (BBC). Film: **American Friends** (Prominent Features). **Deadly Advice** (Deadly Advice Productions).

KEN STOTT - Alceste
Theatre includes: **Henry IV Parts I** and **II, Henry V** and **The Merry Wives of Windsor** (RSC). **The Rose Tattoo** (Playhouse Theatre). **The Beaux Stratagem** (Lyric Theatre, Hammersmith). **American Bagpipes** and **Colquhoun and MacBryde** (Royal Court). **Through the Leaves** (The Bush Theatre). **White Rose** (Almeida Theatre). **Death of a Salesman** (West Yorkshire Playhouse). **The Magistrate, Three Men on a Horse, Jacobowsky and the Colonel, The Tempest, Cymbeline, The Winter's Tale** and **The Sea** (Royal National Theatre). **The Recruiting Officer** for which he was nominated for the 1993 Olivier Award for Best Actor in a Supporting Role and **Broken Glass** for which he won the 1995 Olivier Award for Best Actor in a Supporting Role (also for the Royal National Theatre). Television includes: **King Lear** and **The Beggar's Opera** (directed by Jonathon Miller for the BBC). **The Singing Detective, Bad Company** and **All Good Things** (BBC). **Takin' Over the Asylum** and **Your Cheatin' Heart** (BBC Scotland). **Rhodes** (Zenith), **Silent Witness** and **A Mug's Game** (BBC) to be shown in 1996. Film includes **Franz Kafka's Its a Wonderful Life** (Conundrum Films) which won an Oscar for Best Short Film. **Being Human** (Universal) and **Shallow Grave** (directed by Danny Boyle).

LINDSAY POSNER - Director
As Associate Director at the Royal Court Theatre Lindsay's main house productions include **The Treatment** by Martin Crimp, **Death and the Maiden** by Ariel Dorfman (winner of two Olivier Awards), **Colquhoun And Macbryde** by John Byrne and **American Bagpipes** by Iain Heggie. Royal Court Theatre Upstairs productions include **Ficky Stingers** by Eve Lewis, **No One Sees the Video** by Martin Crimp, **Built on Sand** by Daniel Mornin, **Blood** by Harwant Bains, **Downfall** and **Ambulance** by

Gregory Motton. Other work for theatre includes: **The Lady from the Sea** (The Lyric, Hammersmith and West Yorkshire Playhouse). **The Seagull** (The Gate Theatre, Dublin). **The Robbers** (The Gate Theatre, Notting Hill) **Leonce and Lena** (Sheffield Crucible Studio). **The Doctor of Honour** (Cheek by Jowl - National Theatre tour and then at The Donmar Warehouse). **Much Ado About Nothing** (Regent's Park Open Air Theatre). Television: **The Maitlands** (Performance). **Two Oranges and a Mango** (Stages). Opera: **Jenufa** (Opera Theatre Company).

JOANNA PARKER - Designer
Work for theatre includes: Schiller's **The Robbers** (The Gate, Notting Hill), **The Suicide** (The Beckett Centre, Dublin). Opera: Opera Theatre Company's **Flavio** by Handel (Wexford and The Gate, Dublin). **The Magic Flute** (Royal College of Music). Dance: work for The Cholmondeleys, London Contemporary Dance Theatre and other independent dance projects.

PADDY CUNNEEN - Composer
Paddy is an Associate Director of Cheek by Jowl and has written music for all their productions since 1988. Work for the Royal National Theatre includes: **Fuente Ovejuna, Peer Gynt, The Sea, Angels in America, Sweeney Todd** and **A Little Night Music**. Work for the Royal Shakespeare Company: **The Alchemist, The Changeling, Richard III** and **The Painter of Dishonour**. Other theatre includes: **The Treatment** (Royal Court Theatre), **The Colleen Bawn** (Royal Exchange), **The Lady from the Sea** (West Yorkshire Playhouse), **A Doll's House, The Seagull** (Gate, Dublin), **King of the Castle** (Abbey, Dublin), **Silverlands** (Druid, Galway). **Cabaret** and **Company** (Donmar Warehouse). For television: **The Big Fish** and **The Pan Loaf** (Channel 4). **Oranges and a Mango** and **The Maitlands** (BBC2). As a director: **Slaughterhouse 5** (Liverpool Everyman) and Goldoni's **Il Feudatario** (The Gate, Notting Hill).

SIMON CORDER - Lighting Designer
Simon Corder joined the circus as a ring boy when he left school in 1978. He went on to learn his craft as a technician in touring theatre and opera. In 1981 he joined Lumiere and Son Theatre Company lighting over 20 shows and site-specific performances in the UK and around the world. As a professional photographer in the mid-80's he combined news and arts photography with original images for projection in performance. Recently he designed the lighting for the first night-time zoo in the world: Night Safari in Singapore. Simon's career as a theatrical lighting designer includes over 100 designs for opera, theatre and dance, in situations ranging from Europe's finest Opera Houses to studios at the cutting edge of the avant-garde.

YOUNG VIC COMPANY

The YOUNG VIC gratefully acknowledges the financial assistance of the London Arts Board, the London Boroughs Grants Committee and the London Borough of Lambeth. Box Office sponsored by Digital Equipment Co.

WITH THANKS TO: Orchid Drinks Ltd., Viaduct Furniture Ltd., Bang and Olufsen, champagne by Veuve Clicquot Ponsardin *the champagne of the theatre season*, herbal cigarettes by Honeyrose Products Limited, Stowmarket, Penguin Books, Geographers A-Z Map Company, the Almeida Theatre, Persil Comfort and Stergene courtesy of Lever Brothers for wardrobe care, The End nightclub, 16 West Central Street, WC1, for the sofa, Waterloo Flowers.

For the safety and comfort of patrons smoking is not permitted in the auditorium. In accordance with the requirements of the London Borough of Lambeth persons shall not be permitted to stand or sit in any of the gangways. If standing be permitted in the gangways and at the rear of the seating, it shall be limited to the numbers indicated on notices exhibited in those positions.

Photography or recording is not permitted in the auditorium.

YOUNG VIC COMPANY, 66 The Cut, Waterloo, London, SE1 8LZ.
A company limited by guarantee, registered in England No. 1188209.
VAT Registration No: 236 673348. Charity Registration No: 268876.

Box Office 0171 928 6363
Administration 0171 633 0133
Press Office 0171 620 0568
Fax 0171 928 1585
Textphone 0171 620 1011

Young Vic Funded Ticket Scheme

It is central to the aims of the Young Vic theatre to present adventurous work of the highest quality and so to attract younger audiences into the theatre, to this end ticket prices are kept to a minimum, however, the cost of tickets is still a major barrier for many people. The Young Vic has introduced the Funded Ticket scheme, appealing for funds to enable groups of young people to visit the theatre, often for the first time. During 1995 the scheme has enabled over 2000 children and young people, who would not otherwise have had the opportunity, to experience live drama, and funding is currently being sought to repeat this success in 1996.

The **Funded Ticket Scheme** is a unique venture encouraging audiences of the future. To find out more about the scheme please contact Sophie Byatt, Development Officer on 0171 633 0133.

GRIMM TALES ADAPTED BY CAROL ANN DUFFY
DRAMATISED BY TIM SUPPLE

'*In the true sense of the word, enchanting*' The Guardian

The volume contains Carol Ann Duffy's adaptation and Tim Supple's dramatisation plus drawings by Melany Still, from the production at the Young Vic Theatre at Christmas 1994. Also included are notes for teachers on the staging of the play in schools.

Available from the YOUNG VIC and all good bookshops.
Published by Faber and Faber

From March 1996 the original production of **GRIMM TALES** will be on tour, visiting Festivals in Hong Kong, Australia and New Zealand.

Welcome to a
New Year

Unlike many other theatres, 1996 will
be a genuinely New Year
at the Royal Court.

The Royal Court Theatre's new season
brochure is now available.
Seven new plays plus two Royal Court
Classics in the West End

Call the Box Office now on
0171 730 1745
and full details of the season will be
sent FREE to your home.

The Royal Court:
new plays as classics
and classics as new plays

(since 1956)

Registered charity number 231242

The Almeida Theatre Company Spring Season 1996

8 FEBRUARY – 30 MARCH

"1953"

BY CRAIG RAINE

In an imagined 1953, Fascism dominates Europe,
Hitler is still alive and Mussolini's son rules Italy

DIRECTION PATRICK MARBER   DESIGN VICKI MORTIMER

CAST INCLUDES EMMA FIELDING, JASON ISAACS
ADAM KOTZ AND POUKY QUESNEL

Presented in association with
AT&T OnStage®

AT&T

Almeida
THEATRE

18 April – 15 June

Moliere's

Tartuffe

translated by Richard Wilbur

Orgon (Ian McDiarmid) experiences
a mid-life crisis. Investing Tartuffe –
a charlatan mystic – with saintly powers,
he sacrifices his house, his children and
very nearly his wife to his obsession.

DIRECTION: Jonathan Kent
DESIGN: James Acheson

Supported by the
LAURA PELS FOUNDATION

Almeida Theatre, Almeida Street, Islington, London N1 1TA
Box Office 0171 359 4404

LONDON
ARTS BOARD

ISLINGTON
COUNCIL

Y THE YOUNG VIC COMPANY PRESENTS

28 March - 20 April

Miss Julie

By August Strindberg
In a new version by Meredith Oakes

Directed by Polly Teale
With John Hannah and Susan Lynch

PERFORMANCES

Monday to Saturday 7.30 pm
Saturday Matinees 2.30 pm

BOX OFFICE **0171 928 6363**

Molière

The Misanthrope

in a version by Martin Crimp

for M

*'Il n'y a aucune bienveillance dans
l'écriture, plutôt une terreur.'*
Barthes

Characters

Alceste, a playwright
John, his friend
Covington, a critic
Jennifer, a movie star
Ellen, a journalist
Marcia, a teacher of acting
Julian, an actor
Alexander, an agent

Also required:
A Motorbike Messenger
Simon, a musician

All characters are British, except Jennifer, who is an American.

The time is now, the place is London.

Note: When a slash (/) appears within the text, this marks the point of interruption in overlapping dialogue.

Act One

London.
    The principal room of a suite in a luxury hotel. Doorway to main entrance. Doorway to bedroom.
    Alceste bursts through the main entrance, followed by John.

John
What is it?

Alceste
Please leave me alone.

John
                         What's wrong?
Come on – tell me what the hell's going on.

Alceste
Just leave me alone – I'd be eternally fucking grateful.

John
You could at least listen without getting in a state.

Alceste
                                   I'll
decide what state to be in, thank you.

John
I just don't understand you.
We're supposed to be friends, then you *pick* on me.

Alceste

Friends? Don't make me laugh. Our friendship is *history*.
We used to friends – OK – correct –
but there are limits to what I'm prepared to accept.
And when I see you talking such total shit
I realise I'm dealing with just one more hypocrite.

John

Alceste, don't tell me you're upset ...

Alceste

Upset? That's the best understatement yet.
To do that to a man with no coercion
is a form of social perversion.
You're suddenly kissing this man on both cheeks:
'Darling – haven't seen you for *weeks* –
if there's anything you need at all
don't hesitate (or was it on his mouth) to call'.
But when I ask you what his game is
you can't even tell me what the bastard's name is.
If I was that compromised, Christ knows,
I'd think I'd take a fucking overdose.

John

(*amused*)

Suicide? Really? But isn't that the quintessent
gesture of the moody adolescent?
Will swallowing fifty paracetamol
really make the world morally more acceptable?

Alceste

What's that supposed to be? An example of wit?

John

I'm so pleased you appreciate it.

But come on – for everyone's satisfaction –
tell us your principles of human interaction.

Alceste
Never try to deceive,
and only say what you truly believe.

John
But if a man takes me in his arms
then I have a duty to say how charmed
I am. If he thinks we relate
then I have a moral duty to reciprocate.

Alceste
What total bollocks. Nothing's more effete
than the moral contortions of the self-proclaimed elite.
The slobbering over the ritual greeting,
the bullshit spoken at every meeting
makes me vomit. What kind of morality
makes a fool the equal of a decent man? What kind of
    society?
OK, let's say I let myself be assaulted
by one of these people who swear I can't be faulted –
what's the point them eulogizing my name
if they treat some cretin exactly the same?
I'm sorry I'm sorry but no one in their right mind
wants (or needs) that kind
of praise. That level of sycophancy
is typical of our moral bankruptcy.
If you value everyone equally highly, I'm afraid you'll
    never
have any values whatsoever.
And since you subscribe to the prevailing culture
I dissociate myself from you if as a result you're
keener to lick arses
than make discriminating choices.

I want to be *valued*. I really can't face
people whose embrace
indiscriminately includes the entire human race.

John
But you're part of society – and one of its norms
is to accept the customary forms
of politeness.

Alceste
                Politeness? I'd introduce extreme penalties
for trafficking in false loyalties.
The purpose (it seems to me) of human discourse
should be to exchange our innermost thoughts
and feelings. In other words what I'm asking
is to see the *man* speaking – not the mask.

John
I can think of places where that philosophy
wouldn't get much sympathy.
Besides – with respect to your ideals –
what's wrong with sometimes hiding what you feel?
Would you really tell certain men and women
exactly what you think of them?
Go up to a fellow artist, say, and start
to tear their precious work apart?

Alceste
Absolutely.

John
                So you'd really tell the director at this
                morning's screening
that the film was anodyne, with no political thrust or
    meaning?

4

Alceste
Definitely.

John
    And I suppose you'd find that sinister
and point the finger at interference by a government
 minister.

Alceste
Naturally.

John
  You're joking.

Alceste
     No I'm not.
Not when I've got
so many examples in front of me
of private political and artistic hypocrisy.
I'm enraged. I can't forgive
the way that men and women choose to live.
Everywhere you look: sycophants, compromise,
 hypocrites,
nepotism, betrayal, vested interests –
I've had enough. Call it insanity
but I take issue with the whole of humanity.

John
I have to say that this so-called rage
would make more sense on the seventeenth-century
 stage.
And surely as a playwright you're aware
of sounding like something straight out of Molière.

Alceste
Jesus Christ, you think you're so clever.

5

John

You see, you'll never
change society single-handed. And if it's the truth
    you're after,
the truth is is that ranting moralists are met by ridicule
    and laughter.

Alceste

Exactly. That's just what I'd expect.
It would nauseate me to be treated with respect.

John

Are you saying that humanity should be condemned?

Alceste

I'm saying that humanity as we know it – yes – should
    come to an end.

John

And are we to take it (because I think you're going too
    far)
that no one is exempt from your *fatwah*?
Is it universal, or will there be some / kind of –

Alceste

Universal. I hate everyone.
And not just people in the public eye,
but the public themselves who just stand by
and watch – whose understanding's limited
to absorbing a few selected images.
As you know, I'm in the potentially disastrous position
of allegedly slandering this wretched politician
just by suggesting a 'declaration of his interests'
should include details of his current mistress.
Next thing you know he's posing in his garden
complete with wife, dogs and children

in a grinning parody
of the nuclear family
hoping with the aid of labrador retrievers
to deceive us
into thinking the only people who take lovers
are the poor, the unemployed and single mothers.
And despite this total lack of integrity
he's the one afforded celebrity
status: on the news ...
interviews ...
he's free to choose.
While I'm accused
of being malicious and uncouth
when all I've told's the simple truth.
Jesus wept! And you wonder why
I sometimes want to just curl up and die?
I have a dream of a clean white space
entirely disinfected of the human race.

John

Please
could we just ease
up on contemporary morality
and show a little more understanding of human reality.
Wouldn't it be good to see
some flexibility?
(Or even moral relativity?)
After all, society changes,
and there are whole ranges
of valid responses. Extremes are usually dangerous
and often cause unreasonable pain to us.
We live in a complex social matrix:
nothing's solved by getting back to basics,
Perfection's beyond us. Why can't you just go
with the flow?
If you want to castigate society

then please do it well away from me.
I'm as aware as you are of people's malefactions,
they simply don't provoke the same absurd reactions.
I take people as they come. And if someone acts like a
     shit
then – OK – no problem – let's just quietly deal with it.
You know as well as I do the essential rule
is keep calm, stay cool.

Alceste

You're so reasonable you make me sick.
You'd stay cool while someone sliced off your prick.
What if a close friend betrays you? Or goes 'n
has your assets frozen?
What if they sell your story to the gutter press?
Don't you seek redress?

John

Perhaps. Yes.
But I don't lose my temper. It's hard to be 'enraged'
if one is philosophically disengaged.
And the human animal looks far less fearsome
through the prism
of postmodernism.
The world's a mess. Absolutely. We've fucked it.
So why not just sit back and deconstruct it?

Alceste

So I should allow myself to come to harm
and stay quite calm?
Words can't express my hatred of corrupt men.

John

Why don't you just shut up then.

(*Pause.*)

This court-case of yours, how will you influence the
  outcome?

John

I shan't. I have implicit trust in the process.

John

So who's going to discredit the principal witness?

Alceste

No one. The suggestion's totally / *appalling*.

John

But who's going to photograph the judge kerb-crawling?

Alceste

No one. I have justice on my side.

John

That's the legal equivalent of suicide.

Alceste

No dirty tricks. The way I see it,
it's an open and / shut case.

John

On your own head be it.

Alceste

That's fine.

John

Your litigant's invested
large sums, he has *friends* / who can –

Alceste

I'm not interested.

John

Well you should be.

Alceste

It's my right to choose.

John

I don't think / that's wise.

Alceste

And besides I'm quite happy to lose.

John

You must be / joking.

Alceste

Given our sick and twisted judiciary, I trust this
will become a classic example of perversion of the
    course of justice.

John

You're out of your mind. This is / *insanity*.

Alceste

Losing my case would be a great moral victory.

John

No such thing exists, Alceste. (Really, the stuff you
    spout
would make intelligent people just fall about.)

Alceste

That's their problem.

John
            Really? I think it could well
be yours too. But tell
me something: it seems you're not so inflexible
in your attitude to ... sexual
partners. Not so above it all
you don't notice what's available.
Not so embroiled in your heroic struggle with the
    human race
you fail to recognize a pretty face.
I'm just amazed that you should admire
such an unlikely object of desire.
Ellen, I suspect, is secretly rather fascinated by you.
Marcia can hardly disguise the fact that she's infatuated
    by you
But you don't even speak to them any more
since you became obsessed by Jennifer,
a woman whose distaste for monogamy
is already legendary.
And since she's arrived in London
her door's been open to men almost at random.
She flirts, she slags people off. Is that acceptable
just because she's beautiful?
Ever since she crossed the Atlantic
her life in this hotel has been both frivolous and frantic.
Surely she represents everything you most hate?

Alceste
She's still very young and vulnerable. Don't underrate
love. I know exactly
what her faults are and in a perverse way they attract me.
She takes her success at face value (but then again
that's very American)
and until she gains more insight I'm resigned
(no please don't laugh) to going out of my mind.
My strategy is to let *her* choose

when to reveal her hidden virtues.

John
Hidden is certainly the operative word.
Does she love you?

Alceste
Don't refer
to her like that. Of course she does.

John
So then what's all this fuss
you've been making about her other boyfriends?
    Insecurity?

Alceste
Look: all I ask is a one hundred per cent commitment
    to me.
I've simply come here for an explanation,
and to alert her to the seriousness of the situation.

John
Well I'm sorry, but if you ask me,
Ellen would be a far more likely
candidate. It's the kind of opportunity not to be missed:
sex with a radical post-feminist journalist –
reason enough, surely, to try her.

Alceste
Reason has no influence over desire.

John
You're beginning to worry me. Any
other man would surely ...

(*He sees Covington in the doorway. Slight pause.*)

Covington
                    Hello. I'd arranged to meet Jenny
here after the screening
but a message down at the desk said that now this
    evening
is the earliest she can manage. Pity.
But then they told me
(rather begrudgingly)
that you had use of the key
(Of course that's nothing whatsoever to do with me –
I mean: the key
why should it be?
Obviously.)
But then I thought, well why not take this opportunity
of coming up to see
a man
I've always dreamed of taking by the hand
thereby confirming our friendship
and cementing – dare I say it? Yes I do – a lasting
    relationship.

(*He offers his hand to Alceste who seems unaware of his
existence.*)

    Excuse me I thought we were having a conversation.

Alceste
 ·Really?

Covington
    Or have I misread the situation?

Alceste
You should just be (I'm not sure) just be aware of the
    ·danger
of committing yourself to a complete stranger.

Covington

Well I'm sorry if I startled you,
it's just I've always had the very highest regard for you.

Alceste

Listen –

Covington

Of course (yes, don't say it) there are writers in
        more prominent positions,
but none with the breadth, depth and sheer range of
    your dramatic vision.

Alceste

Listen –

Covington

Believe me, this comes straight from the heart
which is why I'm so anxious to start
a genuine friendship – anticipating that any future
benefits will be mutual.
Let's set up a meeting. Where's your diary?
Shall we do lunch?

Alceste

I'm sorry?

Covington

Is there a problem? Excuse me?

Alceste

A problem? No. Hold on. I'm a little overwhelmed
– that's all – to be claimed as a friend
so suddenly … I mean without any preliminary …
I like there to be a little bit of …
                    (how can I put this?)

Covington

Of mystery?

Alceste

Exactly.

Covington

Of course.

Alceste

It takes *time* / to make –

Covington

Absolutely.

Alceste

– the right choices. I'm afraid I'm (sorry) slightly
fanatical
about friendship. (I mean we may be / quite incompatible.)

Covington

Absolutely – you're absolutely right.
Time – yes – a characteristic, if I may say so, insight
into human nature. Brilliant. Meanwhile if there's anything at all
you need (perhaps a little editorial?)
just call
me at the paper.

(*Produces card.*)

Or look: phone me at home.
I want you to feel that as an artist you're not alone.
We critics are artists too:
perhaps you don't realize just how much I could do for
you.
Who knows – it might even reach the stage

where I could get you on to the front page
– like a Lloyd-Webber musical – or some other natural
   disaster.

(*Laughs at his own joke.*)

OK, OK, you're wondering what I'm after:
well the fact is I have something here
(a play actually)
a script I've been working on for the past year –
and I'd love to get your reaction.

Alceste

(*faint laugh*)

I don't think you'll get much satisfaction
out of me.

Covington
I'm sorry?

Alceste
You'll find
I have the unfashionable habit of speaking my mind.

Covington
Exactly. Good. Yes. I don't want you to be nice:
I'm looking for genuine dramaturgical advice –
I mean if there's anything in particular wrong with it …

Alceste
OK, OK – shall we just get on with it.

Covington
On with it?

Alceste
Read it.

Covington
You mean here? Now? In front of you?

Alceste
Here. Now. Why not? Wouldn't that be fun to do?

(*Alceste grins. Covington opens his script and reads.*)

Covington
'Scene One. Evening. An attic room.' Perhaps I should just say
it's more a scene than a complete play.

Alceste
OK.

Covington
'A man and a woman' – and it's directly based
on my own personal experience.

Alceste
Well that's often the case.

Covington
Exactly. 'Scene One.' Is it? Good. (The man by the way
is me,
there's a strong element of ...)

Alceste
Autobiography.

Covington
Exactly. Yes. Of course there are more scenes planned.

Alceste
Fine. A first draft. I understand.

Covington
'Scene One. Evening. An attic room. A man and a
    woman: Clair.
Clair is young and beautiful.
The man is somewhat older – powerful
but sensitive and aware.'

Alceste
(Of what? Sorry? Is this the play?

Covington
Just aware.

Alceste
Aware. I see. OK.)

Covington
'They look at each other. Silence.'

(*Pause.*)

Alceste
But what are the characters' intentions?

Covington
Those are just the stage directions.

Alceste
(OK. I see.)

John
Two good strong parts.

Covington

Thank you. Now this is where the dialogue starts –
'MAN: My darling, let me crush you in my arms.
WOMAN: I'm no longer susceptible to your monied
charms.
MAN: Make love to me. Forget this girlish nonsense.
WOMAN: I can't. I have a new-found social conscience.
Pause.'

John

Brilliant. I'm hooked. The theme is timeless.

Alceste

(I've never heard anything so completely / mindless.)

Covington

'MAN: Remember all the good times that we had.
WOMAN: The times that you call good now all seem
bad.
MAN: Let's dine out at my restaurant. The limousine is
ready.
WOMAN: I'd rather stay at home and cook my own
spaghetti.
I'd rather stay at home and find out who I am.
MAN: Your name is Clair. And I'm the man
who loves you. Who cares if it's not right!
WOMAN: Oh God! Oh God!
      They kiss beneath the leaking skylight.'

(*Closes the script with satisfaction.*)

There's already interest from the RNT.

John

I'm not surprised. I liked the pause particularly.

Covington

You don't think it owes too much to Pinter?

John

Far from it. There's not even a hint of ...

Alceste

(Talent.)

John

... plagiarism. In fact I don't think I appear t've
heard anything quite like it in the theatre.
Have you, Alceste?

Covington

(*delighted*)

Really?

Alceste

(What?)

Covington

D'you mean it?

Alceste

(I pity the poor bastards who / have to read it.)

John

Of *course* I mean it. The National's sure to / buy it.

Covington

What d'you think, Alceste? You're being very quiet.

Alceste

(*smiles*)

Listen. When someone writes a script
it's very hard for them to stand back from it.
I did in fact once read a scene similar to yours
(admittedly without the pause)
but it did give me cause
to wonder what makes people cover page after page
with dialogue so unplayable on the stage.
Why is there so little insight
into the qualities required to be a playwright?

Covington

If you're talking about what I've just read
to you, I / think you should –

Alceste

                That's not what I said.
No. It was more of a rhetorical question.
Listen. Let me make a suggestion:
If someone has zero facility
it's a disability
they should conceal.

Covington

Zero facility? Is he talking about me?

Alceste

I just said 'someone'. Please don't shout. (You see –
people just have to discuss writing
and they / start fighting.)

Covington

Are you saying I have no talent?

Alceste

I'm not saying anything. Perhaps you have – perhaps
   you haven't.
(Although you can still write total shit
and find some fool to workshop it
book a venue for the evening
and subject your friends to a rehearsed reading.)
Whatever. But please – resist the temptation:
you're not going to get an Olivier nomination
(unless of course it's your own).
As a critic you have a certain reputation –
but would you yourself enjoy critical examination?
It's much easier to face a first night
as a critic than a gibbering playwright.

Covington

Yes, but specifically about my scene –
d'you mean / it's –

Alceste

Your scene is rubbish.

Covington

                    (Uh-huh. You mean the actual / scene.)

Alceste

The way your characters speak is stilted and unnatural.
(The actual scene, yes.)
It's flaccid. The dialogue's weak.
The acid test is to reflect the way that people really
   speak.
'Crush you in my arms'?
'Susceptible to your monied charms'?

Covington

It is a first draft.

Alceste

And you wonder why people laughed?
Listen: if you must write a play
it helps not only to have something to say
but also a way of saying it that arrests us
engages us and tests us.
Your dialogue I'm afraid is the verbal equivalent
of industrial effluent
i.e. the tedious platitudes
of emotionally self-indulgent middle-class attitudes –
the kind of waste
that unfortunately we can't legislate against.
(So he loves her, so she's being mean. / Who gives a fuck?)

Covington

I'm sorry, but it's a contemporary theme.

Alceste

If that's your idea of contemporary
you should be adapting classics for the BBC.
(Being so indifferent to good writing
they'd probably find your work rather exciting.)

(*John laughs.*)

No, I'm quite serious:
that kind of sloppy imprecision's
just what they like on television.

Covington

Well I'm sorry but I've been told it has potential.

Alceste

Well of course it's essential
for you to believe that.
(If you didn't want my opinion you / shouldn't've
asked for it.)

Covington
It's already had several rehearsed readings.

Alceste
Well naturally – people are afraid of hurting / your
  feelings.

Covington
Well-known actors have read these parts.

Alceste
Actors are generous. They have over-kind / hearts.

Covington
Artists are always misunderstood.

Alceste
                              But the hard part is
is the misunderstood are not necessarily artists.

Covington
Well I'd be very interested to see
how you'd handle a similar theme.

Alceste
Listen – if I *had* written such a load of crap
I wouldn't be going round advertising the fact.

Covington
I'd advise you not to adopt that tone.

Alceste
Oh really? Listen: why don't you just leave me alone.
Go home.

Covington

You're arrogant, rude and totally insensitive.

Alceste

And you're becoming increasingly offensive.

John

Please. Both of you. What if she walks in?

Covington

Who? Jennifer? Oh my God have I been
(sorry) shouting? He's right. We'll deal with this (OK?)
another day.

Alceste

Absolutely. And thank you so much for showing us
   your play.

(*Covington goes.*)

John

Congratulations. All he wanted was encouragement
and you turn it into a major incident.
Did you have to make such a big bloody deal of it?

Alceste

Just shut the fuck up / will you.

John

                    Oh charming.

Alceste

                              Hypocrite.

(*Pause.*)

John

I hope you realize …

Alceste

I'm not listening.

John

Fine.

Alceste

Don't interfere.

(*Pause.*)

Realize what?

John

Nothing.

Alceste

Tell me.

John

Only that you've just ended your career.

Alceste

Please. I'm not prepared to discuss the topic.

John

And I'm beginning to find you excessively misanthropic.

Act Two

Alceste, Jennifer.

Alceste
Listen: I'm afraid I'm in a mood
today to question your whole incredible attitude.
You're looking at a man at the end of his tether
who's finding it harder and harder to believe we have a
    future together.
Of course I could lie to you,
but that's something I would never do.
I can't say things I don't believe
although it would be far less painful to / deceive you.

Jennifer
I see. So I've just come back
to listen to – what? – another moral attack?

Alceste
Not an attack. Please. I'm talking about your intimacy
with other men – this open-door policy
which – however much I trust you –
my own nature simply can't adjust to.

Jennifer
Intimacy? Your imagination's hyperactive.
And would you rather I was old and unattractive?
If a man wants to offer me his regards
what do I do? Call in my bodyguards?

Alceste

That's not the point. Clearly you will attract men:
the mistake is to actively encourage them.
The kind of signals you emit
give the impression – how shall I put it? –
that you're fair game.
I'm sorry but it's true. I'm not saying I blame
you (please, that's not what I meant)
but to claim your behaviour's innocent
is certainly contentious
(and probably disingenuous).
Perhaps you'd like to explain
for example why again and again
I find Alexander here. I have great difficulty seeing
why you think he's such a wonderful human being.
Unless a stringy grey pony-tail
contributes to your idea of the perfect male.
Or is his liberal use of moisturizer
some kind of greasy sexual appetizer?
I suppose his loft in Covent Garden
is a real come-on.
I hear he's bought some very interesting pieces
involving the use of animal fleeces,
likes girls to wear bobby socks,
and have sex watched by a dead sheep in a glass box.

Jennifer

(*laughing*)

That's *not true*.
For christsake Alceste, what the hell's gotten into you?
Alex is my agent. He'd sooner read a contract
than attempt high-risk physical contact.

Alceste

Then why can't your 'agent' leave you alone?

Why can't he deal with you on the phone?

Jennifer
You seem to be jealous of the entire male race.

Alceste
Well hasn't the entire male race been invited up to this
    place?

Jennifer
You ought to find that reassuring.
Isn't it just plain boring
to see so many men? Wouldn't it be much more exciting
if there was a favourite I kept on inviting?

Alceste
The favourite is supposed to be me.
(And you wonder why I'm going mad / with jealousy.)

Jennifer
I love you, Alceste. Isn't that enough?

Alceste
That's just a word I'm afraid: 'love'.

Jennifer
Well it's a word I don't use lightly.
(Really I'm not interested in your linguistic / snobbery.)

Alceste
Don't use lightly. Please. Come *on*.
You probably say it to everyone.

Jennifer
Thank you, Alceste. Thank you so much.
Thank you for your kindness, respect and trust.

How charming. But I refuse to be upset.
Let's just say that as far as my love goes, you can forget
it. That way no one can deceive
you but yourself.

Alceste
                    Jesus wept, I don't believe
this. I'd like to tear my obsession
out by the roots. Let me confess
something: d'you think I'm remotely pleased
to be in the grip of this disease-
like thing: love? I hate this role:
this humiliating lack of self-esteem and self-control.

Jennifer
Really? Aren't you used to having feelings?

Alceste
Not when it means dealing
with you, no. My love is incandescent.
I won't be treated like an infatuated adolescent.

Jennifer
I don't understand. Would you rather pick a fight with
    me
or spend the night with me?
You say love, but what you seem
to have in mind's a kind of puritanical *régime*.

(*Phone.*)

Alceste
If you would just – please – stop playing
games, perhaps we could find a way of saying
what we really / feel … (Oh Jesus, I give up.)

Jennifer

(*picks up phone*)

Yes? Who is it? Oh, hi! (It's Julian.) No. Come right up.

Alceste

I thought you wanted to talk
but no – now some arsehole is going to just walk
in here uninvited. Couldn't it wait? Is it so hard to say
to someone: 'No, come back later'?

Jennifer

Julian wouldn't appreciate that.

Alceste

Julian is a spoilt egotistical overrated showbiz brat.

Jennifer

Well exactly. He knows so many people
that offending him's a potentially lethal / exercise.

Alceste

So now you're going to flatter / his ego by –

Jennifer

Please. Don't pretend these things don't matter.
I'm frightened he could interfere
with the natural progression of my career
if I start saying no. These people never manage to do
anything useful – but they can damage you.
To make some kind of issue of it would be insane
(and besides he supplies me with cocaine).

(*Phone.*)

Alceste

Yes yes yes. Always some excuse not to be alone

with me. And now – Jesus Christ – it's the phone
again. There's absolutely no / *privacy*. I thought we'd
agreed.

Jennifer

(*picks up phone*)

Oh hi! Alexander. How *are* you? Come right up.

Alceste

(*makes to go*)

Alexander. That's all I need.

Jennifer

Where're you going?

Alceste

Out.

Jennifer

Please stay.

Alceste

And be humiliated?

Jennifer

But Alceste.

Alceste

No.

Jennifer

Please.

Alceste
I'm sorry but I'm not affiliated
to this particular club.

Jennifer
But just for today.

Alceste
You're being absurd.

Jennifer
How? By asking you to stay?
Why? Is it so unreasonable to request
just a modicum maybe of graciousness?

Alceste
Sit there, you mean, and listen to their trivia.

Jennifer
Please. For me.

Alceste
I've said no.

Jennifer
Just go then if you're so fucking superior.

(*They realize that Julian and Alexander along with John and
Ellen have appeared and witnessed the end of the argument.
Brief silence.*)

Ellen
We met this pair in the elevator.

Jennifer
Ellen. How *are* you?

(*They kiss.*)

Ellen
Are we still OK for the interview?

Jennifer
Absolutely. Looking forward to it.
Julian. Alex. Hi! Can I put you two on hold for just a
    minute.

(*She takes Alceste aside.*)

So. Are you staying?

Alceste
Only if you stop this degrading game-playing.

Jennifer
Please shut up.

Alceste
Then state your position.

Jennifer
You're being embarrassing.

Alceste
Then make a decision.

Jennifer
A *what*?

Alceste
Yes. Them or me.

Jennifer
You are joking.

34

Alceste
Not at all. You forget I'm not frightened of provoking /
  your pet celebrities.

(Alceste moves away as Alex comes up and kisses Jennifer.)

Alex
Well fuck and fuck again. I've just fucked up a crucial
  deal
by offending Tony at the end of our meal.
I automatically offered him a cigarette
and he interpreted this as a personal – and I'm
  absolutely serious – death-threat.

Jennifer
But I'm afraid that's typical. Tony's an object-lesson in
  narcissistic self-obsession.
And since the move to LA, he's become a born-again
non-smoking spa-drinking low-fat high-jog safe-sex
  Californian.

Julian
Talking of self-obsession, I've just spent the last
hour on the phone with Debbie in tears. She just
can't come to terms with the plain
fact that her career is over. But what can you say?

Jennifer
Julian – you're too kind-hearted.
From what I hear it never even started.
The woman's thirty-two and yet
she's still waiting to be offered Juliet.

Julian

(laughs)

  (Oh you bitch.)

Jennifer

(She *told* me.)

Ellen

(*switches on her tape-machine*)

Is it OK to quote you on that?

Jennifer

I'm sorry? Quote what you like, Ellen. It's a fact.

(*Laughter.*)

Ellen

Have you enjoyed working with Philip?

Jennifer

Yes. I think it was an OK relationship.
Phil's quite authoritarian on the set
but still gives you the space to let
yourself be creative. It's just hard not to despise
a man who's always undressing you with his eyes.
I'm immune. But I do pity those young women
who are prepared to play along with him.
So. Yes. I respect his work –
but in personal terms the man's a total jerk-off.

(*Laughter.*)

Ellen

What about Jeanette?

Jennifer

What can I say?
Jeanette is one of the bravest women working in the
    business today.
At least that's what I read
in all your papers – about how she's succeeded

in giving a voice to whatever – to minorities.
But I have it on good authority
that she's intensely homophobic – and never happier
than when she's attacking the so-called 'gay mafia'.

Ellen
Can you comment on her relationship with Leavis?

Jennifer
Comment? I could write you an entire thesis.
Now there's a writer with no imagination
who's still managed to carve out a reputation
for being at the cutting edge
despite having no feeling for form or language.
He gets a team of actors, the backing of some institution
then goes off to 'workshop' a revolution.
The political complexities
of several centuries
are thoroughly investigated for about ten days
– whereupon he flies back home and writes another of
   his dreadful plays.
He patronizes a nation's plight
while the critics praise his compassion and insight.
(I mean is this work political
or just plain parasitical?)

(*Laughter*.)

Ellen
Have you met Morris?

Jennifer
            Abominable.
He thinks of himself as the Delphic fucking oracle.
He delivers diatribes against the state
from the comfort of his mansion in Notting Hill Gate.
And his righteous indignation

37

is matched only by the size of his personal fortune.

(*Laughter.*)

Ellen
How about Clair? Have you been?
I know people rave about her cuisine.

Jennifer
That's right: she collects exotic recipes
and is rightly famous for her dinner-parties.

Alex
Her flambéed *escalopes* are truly amazing.

Jennifer
If only her intellect were equally blazing.
The most interesting subject simply sparks
off a string of utterly banal remarks.

(*Laughter.*)

Ellen
I believe you know Simon.

Jennifer
Yes. Why? Simon is a personal friend of mine.

John
I've heard he's extremely bright.

Jennifer
So bright he'll spend half the night
proving it. Do you *believe* a man
who speaks entirely in epigrams.
Poor Simon. He can't relax. He's ineffectual
because his responses are purely intellectual.
I doubt that he could make *love* to me

without supplying a critical commentary
with footnotes. And when he's taken coke
he starts to babble on about the *baroque*
and how it would've been such ecstasy
to've lived in a previous century
and all that shit. How nothing written today
compares to the music of Lully or Marin Marais
blah blah blah. Which is when of course he starts to
   fumble at my dress
– and promptly loses consciousness.

(*Laughter.*)

Julian

(*with admiration*)

That's Simon so exactly. *God* she's a bitch.

Alex

What you have there, Jenny, is a very special gift.

Alceste

That's it. Go on. I notice your attacks
are only made behind people's backs.
If those people walked into this room
now you'd soon
be all over them with darling this
and darling fucking that.

Alex

Don't accuse us of hypocrisy:
speak to our resident celebrity.

Alceste

But it's you and your entourage
who encourage
her. It's your pseudo-conviviality

that feeds her taste for this point-scoring triviality.
She might be less sarcastic
if she was deprived of her enthusiastic
audience. Flattery
destroys an individual's critical faculty.

John
But doesn't this all sound rather familiar?
Aren't your pet hates actually rather similar?

Jennifer
Yes, but contradiction is
this man's *vocation*. His
reputation is such that he'd
lose face if he was seen to agree
with anyone – let alone me.
He's so in love with the idea of a fight
that the left half of his brain is at odds with the right.
And if someone *else* expresses an opinion he shares,
then that's it:
he attacks it.

(*Laughter.*)

Alceste
Yes, yes – very funny. But then in this company I'd be
surprised
not to find myself satirized.

John
But come on: admit
you're genetically predisposed to contradict.
It's a sickness. He gets equally mad
if you call something good or the same thing bad.

Alceste
That's because people are always wrong.

The sickness is they've no idea what's really going
   on.
Their critical criteria are rubbish. All
their judgements are entirely superficial.

Jennifer
Oh, *please* ...

Alceste
Please what? Don't you realize
you're just an amusing object in these men's eyes?
OK. It's very entertaining. But you should try
asking what they say about you in private.

Alex
(*smoothly*)

Listen: it would be neither professional nor gallant
– he's lying, darling – for me to rubbish my own best
   client.

Julian
What can I say?
You know we all love you. You're a babe.

Alceste
Don't you see they're just bullshitting you?
I may be upsetting you
but at least that's a function of my sincerity.
I hate to see
you living at this skin-deep level
never taking the time or trouble
to question what your life's really about.
I mean why can't you just throw these people *out*?

Jennifer

(*upset*)

> Sincerity? Don't you just mean
> you want to make an unpleasant scene?
> Your program of instruction apparently depends
> on insulting both myself and my closest friends.

(*to Ellen*)

> Are you still taping this?

Ellen

> If you don't mind. I think it's shaping
> into a very interesting piece,
> and it's the unguarded moments like these
> that are so revealing
> about what my subjects are really experiencing and
>   feeling.
> If I didn't believe you were the new female icon
> I wouldn't've dared to leave the mic on –
> but you see I find your sexual politics
> fascinating. It seems the trick is
> to surround yourself with men
> and yet have no specific psychosexual need for them.
> Am I right? And of course you don't have to answer me
> but I also get this so so weird seventeenth-century
> feel from all of this. It's like I'm in a room of stock
> characters. It's not post-modern, it's *baroque*.
> It's quite unsettling, but then again
> perhaps this is the style of the new millennium:
> a pre-enlightenment sense of linguistic formality
> coupled with post-post-industrial virtual reality.

(*Everyone looks at her.*)

> (… Or something like that.)

Alceste
Well if you want my opinion …

Jennifer
Haven't we already had it?

Alceste
I beg your pardon?

Jennifer
Would anyone like to see the wonderful roof-garden?

(*to Alex and Julian*)

What, are you leaving?

Julian
Are we?

Alex
Of course not.

Alceste

(*to Jennifer*)

That would put you in something of a spot
wouldn't it. It would mean you were free
to speak to me.

Julian
I've got nothing till this afternoon.
What about you? Are you going soon?

Alex
Me? I don't need to get away
until our office opens in LA.

43

Julian

(When's that?)

Alex

(4p.m. our time.)

(*Phone.*)

Jennifer

(*over previous two lines*)

Why are you behaving like this?

Alceste

I'm just trying to test your priorities.

Jennifer

(*picks up phone*)

Yes? Hello? I see. So he's on his way.
OK.
It seems there's a young man in a leather jacket
coming up to deliver an urgent packet
to Alceste.

Alceste

I don't think that's at all likely.

Jennifer

But he asked for you at the desk – one of these ...
  motorbike
people ...

Ellen

Courier.

44

Jennifer
Courier. Thank you.

(*The Messenger appears – long hair, beard, leathers.*)

Oh my
he's here already. (*to Alceste*) Now just try
and be nice to him.

Messenger
Package for Alceste.

Alex
Please. Come in.

Messenger
If you could just sign here and print your name before
you take …

Alceste

(*doing so*)

OK, OK. Are you sure this isn't a mistake?

(*He signs and takes the 'package' – a letter – to one side,
opens it and reads. Jennifer meanwhile intercepts the
Messenger.*)

Jennifer
Don't you get hot in all that leather?

Messenger
Depends. Y'know. On the weather.

Alceste
Jesus wept.

Julian
Bad news?

Alceste
I don't believe it.

(*to John*)

Just look at that. The bastard. Take it. Read it.

(*John takes the letter.*)

Jennifer

(*takes biker's arm*)

What is this? You're upsetting our visitor.

John

(*faint laugh*)

I don't understand. It's from Covington's solicitor.
He's threatening to sue for defamation ...

Jennifer
Have I missed something?

John
... unless he gets a full retraction
of the quote 'malicious attack' unquote on his play
in progress.

Alceste
He's not going to get away
with this.

John
He claims to be suffering mental distress
and loss of earnings as a direct consequence.

Jennifer

You mean Covington the *critic*?
That's ridic-
ulous.

John

Nevertheless it might be sensible to compromise.

Alceste

What? You want me to tell lies?
I'm going to fight.
This is a man who destroys writers' reputations
  overnight.
Mental distress? No way will I praise
his crappy little stabs at writing so-called plays.

John

I still think you should / calm down.

Messenger

Uh … Is there a reply?

Alceste

Yes there is. Tell him I'd rather die
than retract. And you can pass on
the message that his reviews aren't fit to wipe my arse
on.

(*to Alex and Julian who are trying not to laugh*)

And perhaps you two would like to explain
just what you both find so / entertaining.

Messenger

So. OK. Shall I wait while you / write that down?

47

Alceste

(to Jennifer)

And don't think I've forgott-
en our previous conversation. *(to Messenger)* What?

Messenger
I said: shall I wait while you write that down?

Alceste
No. You can find another helmet and bike me into
town.

Act Three

Alexander, Julian.

Alex
You always look so unconcerned.
I wish I could've learned
to be like you. I'm fascinated. You seem blessed
with perfect equanimity. Don't you ever get depressed?

Julian
What about?

Alex
(Because I do.)

Julian
                    There's no secret:
what you see, Alex, is what you get.
Mummy's famous – so is Dad. Of course I've taken
    some trouble
to get noticed – but it's hardly been a struggle.
The transition from teenage idol
to stage and film was painless, so I think I'm entitled
to feel fairly pleased with myself:
I've got work, women, prestige, *ridiculous* (at my age)
    wealth.
I've experimented with guilt, but I'm afraid self-doubt
just doesn't suit me. I'm bright, I'm talked about,
and I have got talent
(and I could name others in my position who haven't).
Basically what it means

is I've inherited all the useful genes
get all the attention in my scenes
and feature regularly in the Sunday magazines.
Worrying about what to wear is the closest
I ever come to what might be called neurosis.
Oh – and my teeth: if I do have a failing
it's my obsession with a three-monthly clean and
    descaling.
But depression? You're joking. I wouldn't want to be
anything other than what I am. (I have no problems
    mentally.)

Alex
Nevertheless you appear
to be wasting your time here.

Julian
D'you really think so? No, I don't invest
my energy unless I'm confident of success.
I'm not one of these pathetic men
who thoroughly degrade themselves when
it comes to women. Anguish
and so on is not my style. The language
of love – let's face it –
is really pretty bloody basic.
I'm making an investment here and expect to earn
a very comfortable return.
I gamble – of course – but I always win:
I always take out more than I put in
(if you get my meaning) – and the clincher
is: to sleep with me would be something of a coup for
    her.
But what about you? I bet you're
after her yourself, you old lecher.

Alex

I take a purely paternal interest.

Julian

Oh yes? And does that extend to incest?

(*Both laugh.*)

Alex

OK. But I still think you're being rather blinkered.
I'd advise you to think hard
about this.

Julian

Blinkered? Oh, absolutely.

Alex

Jennifer's – listen – very astute. She
gives nothing away – unless she's said ...

Julian

What?

Alex

... something to you. Has she?

Julian

Only 'come to bed'.

Alex

Bullshit.

Julian

Well that was the implication.

Alex

Implication bullshit. It's all in your imagination.

No – are you *serious*?

Julian
I'm as serious as you are.

Alex
Stop. Listen. This isn't getting either of us very far.
Are you fucking her – or not?

(*Pause.*)

Julian
Not.

Alex
OK.

Julian
Lunch is as far as I've got –
even then she turned up late
and spent the whole hour pushing steamed broccoli
 round her plate.

Alex
Then listen: you're a betting man
aren't you. Yes? OK, then here's the plan:
Prove to me you've had her – your word is sufficient –
and I'll waive my next six months' commission.
But, if you're the loser
and I seduce her,
then I pay my next six months' rent
by taking an additional 10 per cent.
Do we have an agreement?

Julian
But that's obscene. How can you put such a disgusting
 take on it?

I couldn't. No. (*lowers voice*) She's coming. OK. Quick, let's shake on it.

(*They shake hands as Jennifer enters.*)

Hi.

Jennifer
So. What are you two up to?

Alex
Oh. Nothing.

Jennifer
Is that why Julian's blushing?

(*Pause. Phone.*)

Excuse me.

Julian
(*sotto voce*)

Have I gone really red?

Alex
(*sotto voce*)

Idiot.

Jennifer
(*picks up phone*)

Hello? Well stop her. Say I'm sick in bed or something. OK, OK, I realize it's not your fault.

Alex
Is there a problem?

Jennifer

It seems that Marcia's called
and is on her way up here. I gave express
instructions she wasn't to get past the front desk.

Julian

I'm out of here. That woman's unbearable.
Alex, are you coming?

Jennifer

That's not very charitable.
Surely you're not leaving when
you know how much she enjoys the company of bright
    young men?
She probably knows you're here –
how's she going to feel if you just up and disappear?
No wonder she's incredibly bitter
if this is the way you're going to treat her.
This is a woman who's lonely and damaged,
who's never even managed
to keep a partner. She needs therapy
but hides instead behind an ideology
of outmoded feminist
rhetoric. And because Alceste once kissed
her (they were both drunk) at a first night
party, she now thinks she has some kind of right
over him – which is basically why she hates me
and tries to stir up serious shit against me.
I used to respect her as a teacher – but there's a glitch
– she's become a totally intolerable malicious …

(Marcia appears.)

                                                    … which

way did you come up? Security
has only just this minute gotten on to me.

(They kiss.)

Marcia

The stairs, darling. I'm trying to take more exercise.

Jennifer

But this is such a wonderful surprise!

Marcia

(to the men)

Pleased to meet you.

(But the men slip out.)

Don't they believe in protocol?

Jennifer

Drink?

Marcia

No thank you. You know I never touch alcohol.

(Jennifer pours herself a big drink.)

Jenny, I've always (as you know) had a great deal of
   respect for you
which is why I'm not afraid to be direct with you
about your work. When I taught you at Julliard
you were the star student. It wasn't hard
to predict your success. But what really struck everybody
was your fantastic integrity.
But since this last film's come out, there are influential
   (as I'm sure you know) voices
highly critical of your artistic choices,
and I've learned
enough to be really rather deeply concerned.

People are saying (and if you knew how much it hurts
    me)
that what you're doing is just one step from
    pornography.
Yes. They're saying you're an artistic coward
to consistently play women who are disempowered
or psychotic.
Of course I pointed out that what you're doing is erotic
not exploitative. But I sensed
they weren't too convinced by that defence.
And although I far from agreed
I did (under the most enormous pressure) have to
    concede
that your image on the screen
may be (possibly) undermining women's self-esteem,
that they have a right (yes) to be disappointed
if you even *appear* to be exploited,
that your style of living
(I mean look at it)
is not an appropriate model for today's women.
Listen: I'm not saying you've sold out,
I'm just saying I'm worried about
you. You're not corrupt, but be aware that you're
entering a morally grey area.
I know that you're sufficiently intelligent
to realize that this advice is well-meant.
And I wouldn't've even mentioned it
if I didn't feel we had a very special relationship.

Jennifer

Well thank you, Marcia. You've given me a great deal
to think about. And I feel
that far from taking offence (as one might) at what you
    say,
I'd prefer to instantly return the favour.
And since you've shown such great integrity

56

by repeating what's said about me,
the very least that I can do
is repeat (much as it pains me) what people say about
    you.
I threw a party here the other night for intellectuals
(including I may say radical homosexuals
of both camps). And I hope I'm not betraying anyone's
    trust
to say that you were discussed.
People said that your attitude to (so-called) pornography
would be funny
if it wasn't so deeply reactionary.
They attributed your need to criticize and interfere
to the exemplary mediocrity of your own career
(I think that was the phrase)
and suggested that jealousy
and confused sexuality
might be at the root of what they called the banality
of your opinions. *Professionally* you were accused of
    muscling in
on actors' work (like Lee Strasberg did to Marilyn)
– trying to maintain a niche
for the discredited techniques you teach.
It was so distressing to hear you abused –
particularly when the word 'dinosaur' was used.
More than one of those present
claimed to've been sent
letters by you suggesting liaisons
for distinctly unprofessional reasons.
Finally it was suggested (surely in error)
that the scenes you condemn in the cinema
are the ones you'd like to see in your own bedroom
    mirror.
Naturally I leapt to your defence
and tried to prevent this (my God it was *intense*)
onslaught from developing. But I was a lone

voice. (And the tone
was far from friendly,
believe me.)
They felt that you lacked insight
and acted principally out of spite.
They claimed your long-standing grudge meant
you were disqualified from objective judgement.
So maybe it would be (don't you think) wise
to be a little less quick in future to criticize?
I *think* that you're sufficiently intelligent
to realize that this advice is well-meant.
And I wouldn't've even mentioned it
if I didn't feel we had a very special relationship.

Marcia
Of course I expected
insults, but not to be subjected
to this. I'm all the more disturbed,
Jennifer, because I've so obviously touched a nerve.

Jennifer
Oh really? No, I think we should start
to have these heart-to-hearts
more regularly. Far from being frightening
I find it very very enlightening.
Let's do a deal:
how would you feel
if we agreed
to always report what's said about you and what's said
   about me?

Marcia
What? Act as your private detective
in return for more lies and invective?

Jennifer

You see, I'm sure the moral values we apply
undergo subtle changes as the years roll by.
And what one person sees as a celebration
of the body, another sees as cynical exploitation.
Perhaps the work I do now will seem outrageous
when I've reached middle-age as
you've done, and have a chance to re-assess.
I do appreciate your maternal interest:
but life must be pretty empty
if you're not allowed to be wild at twenty.

Marcia

Age is irrelevant. This society
is a male-led *as you well know* capitalist conspiracy
which undervalues woman's function
except as teenage objects for immediate sexual
    consumption
on every poster and magazine cover.
Besides, what makes you think I'm old enough to be
    your mother?

Jennifer

What makes *you* think you have a right
to even be here? As it is I'm being polite,
but I could pick up that phone
and have you thrown
out. Yes. Don't you see: you are totally alone.

(*Pause.*)

I am the complete focus of all attention.
And if for reasons too ... unbearable to mention
you can't handle it, I'm sorry. But the media's
fascination with me isn't my fault. They need an
icon. You heard her say it. And as for my body,
I intend to remain its sole authority.

59

If your own is subject to the influence of time,
then that's your problem, I'm afraid, not mine.

Marcia
I never thought I'd live to see the day
Jennifer when you could talk that way
about a friend. Throw me out?
Listen young lady, it's about
time you confronted one or two home truths
about your career. I'm afraid you stand to lose
not just your integrity
and your dignity
but also any vestige of personal privacy.
Who's really in control? Can't you see you've been
sucked into the publicity machine
and spat out as pure product?
Are you really so completely mind-fucked
as to think there's some connection between your fame
    and your own ability?
No, you're just a brand of femininity
to be sold. Your face
is just one more image in the market-place,
and your body
is pure commodity.
Stars aren't born, my darling, they're made
in the world of capital and trade.
The question's not whether your name's up in lights,
the question is: who owns the rights?

Jennifer
But if it's so easy to become a star
then how very strange it is that you are
a what? A nobody?

Marcia
Careful,

or I shall be forced to descend to your level.

(*Alceste enters unseen by the two women.*)

Oh I know I'm not welcome here
and you'd prefer me just – like your conscience – to disappear.

Jennifer

(*sees Alceste*)

Not welcome? But it's been delightful.
You are a true friend. Alceste, she's *so* insightful
and what I particularly admire
is that very special wisdom you can only acquire
with age.

(*She puts her arms around them both and leads them downstage.*)

Listen, do promise me you'll both be wearing
the wonderful costumes I've been preparing
for this evening's little party. The theme's Louis
Quatorze –
the kind of thing an American in Europe just adores.

(*Pause.*)

Look, why don't I leave the two of you to have a talk.
It's one o'clock. I promised I'd call my parents in New
York.

(*Jennifer goes into the bedroom. Silence.*)

Marcia

(*faint laugh*)

Louis Quatorze?
In the old days this would be the scene where I wait for
my carriage

while we discuss things like 'love' and 'marriage'.

(*Pause.*)

> I can't tell you how much your work means
> to me. You write the kinds of scenes
> that mysteriously reveal the human
> condition. And particularly as a woman
> I feel drawn to you. I only wish
> your work was better known. Rubbish
> gets all the attention. You ought to be a household
>   name.

Alceste

I like to think I have at least a modicum of fame.
And for the moment
at least, it's proportional to my actual achievement.

Marcia

But you're much too modest. People get famous
for achieving far less.
A real artist like yourself may not know how to seize
the relevant opportunities
which I / might be able –

Alceste

                Please God, don't let's start
a conversation about what is or is not art.
Besides, what major institution
isn't in a state of abject aesthetic confusion?

Marcia

Yes, but true art makes its own conditions.
I know people in powerful positions
who speak very highly of you
– no – really – they do.

Alceste

People will speak highly of a pile of shit
if they've dressed up and spent fifty quid to see it.
I mean could you really bear
to sit through another play by Alan Bennett or David
    fucking Hare?
Or watch an audience gratefully reacting
to yet another *tour de force* of classic over-acting?

(*C'est un scélérat qui parle.*)

Marcia

Be careful who you attack.
(Is it legal to use real people's names like that?)
No, you'd be surprised
at who I know. Without being at all compromised
you're welcome to use
my connections in any way you choose.

Alceste

I'm afraid what you're
suggesting is anathema.
I just haven't been designed
to get down on my knees and lick unwiped behinds.

(*Marcia makes a face.*)

You see: if what I say disgusts
you then how could you possibly trust
me with your friends. When I select an epithet
I'm not concerned with things like etiquette.
My chronic inability to dissimulate
means I'm fated
to be excluded from the centres of power
with all the advantages they can confer.
So – yes – I break the rules,
but at least I don't have to suffer the company of fools.

Marcia

Yes. Well. I see it's a sensitive subject.
What interests me more is what exactly is the object
of your visits here? I assume you're not … emotionally
involved? If so you've no notion
of what you're dealing with. A man with your panache
deserves better than a piece of transatlantic trash.

Alceste

That's an extraordinary thing to say
about someone you claim
as a friend.

Marcia

Perhaps. Only I'm concerned
you're going to get your fingers very badly burned.
It hurts me to see you so obsessed
when you're not (as you probably know) her principal
    interest.

Alceste

What's that supposed to mean?
What exactly has she been / saying to you?

Marcia

She may be my friend, but that doesn't make her
yours, darling. She's all on the surface. Don't take her
at face value.

Alceste

I refuse to believe she's intrinsically shallow.
And I don't see
what the point is of trying to upset me.

Marcia

Fair enough. I'll draw my own conclusions

then and leave you to your romantic illusions.

                    Alceste
Come back. No. Marcia. Wait.
What can you do to substantiate
your accusations? You can't plant the seeds of doubt
like that and just walk out.

                    Marcia
Can't I?

(Pause.)

          Alright. Then step this way
and I'll show you my exhibit A.
Come back to my flat with me
and you'll find out everything you ever needed to know
    about infidelity
(hers I mean) but were afraid to ask.
Come on. The world's not going to fall apart.
But if it does I'll offer you what consolation
I can by way of compensation.

Act Four

Ellen, John.

John

It was the most incredible sight:
he jumps off the motorbike – right? –
and immediately starts hammering on Covington's
   door.
Covington appears in shock at the first-floor
window and tells him to fuck off or he'll call the police
(I'm parked at the end of the street just in case).
Alceste says, 'You told me to call you at home
you bastard, and here I am.' 'I'm phoning
them now,' says Covington. Slams the window shut.
   Silence.
There's this feeling of potential violence.
Then the door opens: Covington grins
(a new tactic) says, 'Listen, why don't you come in
and discuss this.' (Although the door's still on the
   chain.)
'No,' says Alceste. 'I'll say what I have to say
out here. I've nothing against you as a man
or as a journalist – I've even been a fan
of yours in that capacity –
but please have the sagacity
to see that writing reviews is a world apart
from writing plays – which is: Art.
I gave you my sincere opinion, and issuing a writ
against me isn't going to alter it.'
Well Covington looks as if he's going to burst
into tears. Perhaps that's why Alceste

66

becomes amazingly (for him) polite.
'Let's shake hands,' he says. 'It's not dignified
to turn this into a vendetta.
After all, your play does have almost infinite potential
   to be better.'

(*Ellen laughs.*)

Poor Covington can't argue any more, but
quickly shakes his hand and clicks the door shut.

Ellen
He certainly knows how to create a scene.
It's almost touching – d'you know what I mean? –
for a man still to believe that words like 'dignified'
are not just signs, that what is signified
by 'love' or 'sincerely'
can exist independently of literary theory.

John
Yes, and he's particularly Quixotic
in the way he sentimentalizes the erotic.
His attitude to gender shows no respect
for any of the more important texts.
He still treats Jenny
as if she was his own personal property.

Ellen
I know. It's shocking.
I sometimes wonder if he's mocking
us: seeing just how far he can go
with a perfect simulacrum of machismo.

John
D'you think she believes in 'love' as such?

Ellen

Jenny? I don't think she 'believes' in much
at all. She's far too intelligent
not to question –
but at the same time far too confused
to see the subtle ways in which she's being abused.

John

It worries me to see *him* drawn in
to this situation. I've tried to warn him
off. I even suggested – just as an experiment –
that he might well benefit
– I suppose as a kind of re-education –
from having a relationship
with you.

Ellen

(*amused*)

      Really? Do you always recommend me
then for sexual therapy?
Listen: what the two of them get up to
is their business. Yes, I'd love to
see them both happy at least
(although I am in the process of publishing a piece
which suggests that's unlikely). But as
for offering myself as a consolation prize,
experimentally or otherwise,
I'm not
sure that I've got
the nerve to be that pro-active
(nor, I have to say, do I find him remotely attractive).

John

Well just be warned. In his present
state of mind he's likely to resent

any hint of rejection. And to me
you look like perfect material for his next obsessive
    fantasy.
Of course things may still work out between them
in which case we may even see them
an item yet. And if they do become a pair
then assuming you're not involved elsewhere
and can commit to it intellectually,
perhaps the two of us could …

Ellen

(*amused*)

> Could *what*? Are you coming on to me?

John

Now that's a question
I'd rather was answered by a semiotician.
To do it justice we'd really need a
Roland Barthes or Jacques Derrida.

(*They're both laughing as Alceste enters in intense but suppressed rage.*)

Alceste

Where is she?
How dare she
humiliate me.

Ellen

It's not the end of the world already?

Alceste

The end of the world would be
preferable … I'm going to do something violent
in a moment.
Where the hell is she? (I can't even *think* / straight.)

Ellen

I'm afraid she's not here. Calm down.
                        Get him a drink for / Godsake.

Alceste

How can someone so beautiful
have no sense at all of what is moral?

Ellen

What? Is there a / connection?

Alceste

                        It's a total inversion
of values. It's disgusting. It's perversion.
Jennifer. After all the assurances she gave me ...
Jennifer. Jennifer. Jennifer has betrayed me.

Ellen

Isn't this all rather possessive?

John

(*hands Alceste a drink*)

Please don't be so aggressive.
Come on now. Perversion? What is this?

Alceste

Why don't you just mind your own fucking business.

(*Gulps the drink.*)

I've just been given a tape on which is her own
    profession
of guilt – a confession
(if you can possibly imagine a woman loving him)
of her relationship – yes – with Covington.
The man I thought she found so numbingly boring

70

turns out to be chief client of her compulsive whoring.

John
Using that kind of language
can only exacerbate – don't you see – the damage.

Alceste
Don't tell me Mr Self-Abuse
the words I can or cannot use.

Ellen
But he's right. This vocabulary is problematic.

Alceste
OK then. Let's stop talking and get pragmatic.
If she's capable of gross betrayal
and all the pain that entails,
I'm prepared to reciprocate –
assuming it's not too late
that is to take up your offer.

Ellen

(*glancing at John*)

Offer? I'm sorry?

Alceste
To become my lover.
John's right. A calculated gesture
like that will really test her
nerve. When she sees me transfer my attention
onto you she'll regret ever seeing that unmention-
able little man.
Sweet revenge. You're right. It's the perfect plan.

(*A slight pause as Alceste pours himself another drink. He continues to drink heavily throughout this act.*)

Ellen

Listen … I realize you're upset. But that said
(and maybe the drink's gone to your head
or whatever) I'm not aware of any such 'plan'.
Unless John (what exactly have you been saying?) can
perhaps elucidate?
(Thank you so much, John.) But at any rate
surely this so-called 'love' of yours
should make you blind to whatever flaws
she may have. Isn't that what every cliché teaches us
from Marcel Proust back to Lucretius?

Alceste

There's no question of forgiving her.
This is life, not literature.
I intend to make
a complete break.

(*He drinks, self-absorbed, and doesn't notice that Jennifer is
in the room looking questioningly at Ellen and John.*)

Ellen

(*quietly amused to Jennifer*)

Things seem to be more than he can bear.

John

Come on. Let's see what we're going to wear.

(*as they go out*)

Look, I'm so sorry if I embarrassed you …

Ellen

Don't worry. I was just a little bit surprised, that's all …

(*They've gone, laughing softly. Jennifer comes right into the room. Alceste, of course, now knows she's there, but remains punishingly silent, nursing his drink.)*

Jennifer
Has something happened? Are you angry?
I get the impression you're mad at me.

Alceste
(Give me strength.)

Jennifer
I'm sorry?

Alceste
       I said:
Give me strength. So what's he like in bed?

Jennifer
What?

Alceste
   Still critical? Or does he lose his objectivity
during exquisite sexual activity?
Was it in this apartment?
I'm beginning to find you physically and morally
   repugnant.

Jennifer
(strokes his cheek)

Come on. I bet you say that to all the girls.

Alceste
How can you joke about it? The world
you inhabit turns betrayal into a game
– only there are no rules, and no sense of shame.

73

You've just amused yourself with me
(of course, I instinctively
knew that, and everything she's said
confirms things I already
suspected). But I had no real conception
that such effortless deception
was innate.
I warn you: you've chosen the wrong person to
    humiliate.
I accept that you have every right
to love who you like, to spend the night
with who you like. Love – clearly – can't be forced
on someone any more than it can be divorced
from passion. Yes – I understand desire –
but not the chronic need to be a liar.
What was it you said to me?
'Love is a word I don't use lightly'?
If that's the case
then not just love but life itself is meaningless:
and we reach the terminal stage
where there's no feeling left – only rage.
I feel physically sick
just at the thought of it.
You have no soul.
(I think I'd better leave before I lose control.)

Jennifer
Leave? You can't make serious (I assume) accusations
then just walk out of the situation.

Alceste
Really? I should've walked out of this
the moment I became suspicious
instead of falling even more in love
and being made a complete fool of.

Jennifer

You're intriguing me. I'm completely unaware
of what I've done.

Alceste

How can you stand there
and deny the truth
when I have proof?

(*He goes to the phone, removes the cassette from the
answering machine and inserts another one from his pocket.
He switches it on. After the beep we hear Jennifer's voice –
in contrast to her usual style, she sounds hesitant and vulnerable.*)

Jennifer's Voice

(*breath*) It's me. Are you there? (*breath*) Look, I really
need to talk. (*breath*) I feel very alone here and
you're my only friend. (*breath*) I just wanted to hear
your voice. Sorry. OK. Call me.

(*Alceste switches off the machine. Slight pause.*)

Jennifer

Where did you get that? You have / no right to –

Alceste

(*faint laugh*)

Look at you. You've gone completely white.

Jennifer

Who gave you that? Have you been tapping the phone?

Alceste

(*mocking*)

'My only friend', 'I feel so alone'.

75

Jennifer

Have you?

Alceste
You admit it's your voice.

Jennifer
Yes. Of course. Do I have any *choice*?

Alceste
You admit you're having a relationship
with this man – not just a friendship.

Jennifer
Yes. No. What man? You're going too fast for me.

Alceste
Come on, come on: are you asking me
to believe this loving tone
isn't exclusively reserved for our friend Covington?

Jennifer
Covington? (*faint laugh*) I totally fail to understand.

Alceste
My source is impeccable. *And*
it took a great deal of persuasion
believe you me to obtain this information.

Jennifer
Wait a minute.

(*Slight pause.*)

I realize you've somehow gotten this from Marcia ...
But isn't it obvious the message is for her?

Alceste

Oh absolutely. Yes. Obvious.
Please accept my humble apologies.
How dare you insult my intelligence
by twisting the evidence!
Are you really going to try and distort this ... text
of yours to suggest
you'd be so vulnerable and intimate
with a woman you're widely known to hate?
Well? Shall we listen to it again
while you / attempt to –

Jennifer

I could never explain
anything to you. How dare you assume you have the
   authority
to invade my privacy?

Alceste

Alright, alright.
Calm down. Let's see you try and shed a favourable
   light / on this.

Jennifer

You don't own me. It doesn't matter
to me *what* you think. (Don't flatter / yourself.)

Alceste

OK. I'm sorry. Look; just say
what would make you talk to Marcia that way.

Jennifer

(*coldly and calmly*)

No. It's for Covington.
I've fallen head over heels in love with him.

You're right: he's well-bred
well-read
exquisite (how did you guess?) in bed.
In fact I agree with everything you've said.
Just leave me alone – alright –
then I can get on with fucking every man in sight.

(*Alceste slaps her face.*)

You know something: you're completely mad.
I've just lost any respect I ever had
for you. Your assumption of betrayal
is so predictably male
and your resort to violence
speaks volumes. No. Please. Silence
is infinitely preferable to hearing
                                        how ashamed et cetera et cetera
you now are.
Y'know, what's so endearing
is for me to realize
you've assumed from day one I've been telling lies:
my most intimate confession
of love has been treated throughout with paranoia and
    suspicion.
I tell you I'm in love with you
but, oh no, nothing's ever good enough for you
(and you wonder why I feel isolated and alone
and leave pathetic messages on that woman's phone).
I'm angry.
And I have every right to be.
I naively make a commitment
and in return this is the treatment
I get. (*bitterly*) They say what I do is pornography
– so why don't I stimulate that jealousy
of yours. Yes – why don't I see whether
I can't call some nice young boy right now so you can
    watch us making out together.

78

Alceste

There's nothing remotely naive
about you. D'you really expect me to believe
this victim acting? Don't you see.
you are my destiny.
I shan't let go:
however low you sink I'm going to follow.

Jennifer

That's not love, it's a psychiatric *disorder*.

Alceste

Maybe, maybe it borders
on it, yes. Sometimes I think the whole idea
of love is mad. The fear
of betrayal, of rejection – the reckless pursuit
of one's own personal humiliation. But the root
goes too deep.
I wish there was a way of keeping
you entirely to myself. Imagine if you were blind,
say, or paralysed. You'd find
out how loyal I was, because then
there'd be no other men
sniffing around. I'm the only one you see who wouldn't
  hurt you
or immediately desert you.
I'd have no rival
and you'd depend on me – literally – for your survival.
Where're you going?

Jennifer

        You're frightening me.
What kind of weird fantasy
is that?

Alceste

Jennifer.

Jennifer

No.

Will you please let go
of me.

(*He lets go. Pause.*)

You've had too much to drink.

OK?

(*She backs away.*)

So please: just leave me alone and give me time to
think.

(*She turns suddenly and goes into her bedroom. Alceste
swallows the remainder of his drink.*)

Act Five

Darkness.

A figure appears carrying a lighted candelabrum. He's dressed as a servant at the court of Louis XIV. He moves round the room and lights more candles.

As the light grows we see that the hotel room has been transformed – by hangings and ornaments – into the baroque. There is an open harpsichord with an erotic painting inside the lid.

As the servant figure – Simon – moves downstage he finds Alceste slumped asleep in a chair. Simon shakes him gently.

Simon
Monsieur? Monsieur?

(Alceste wakes up.)

Alceste
What the fuck ... ?

Simon

(mysteriously)

                          Voici bien des mystères.

(Pause.)

Alceste
Who are you?

Simon
Nous sommes mal, Monsieur, dans nos affaires.

Alceste

I don't speak French. Why are you dressed
like that? I'm sorry but I'm not impressed.

Simon

Monsieur, il faut faire retraite.

Alceste

What?

Simon

Il faut d'ici déloger sans trompette.

Alceste

Speak to me in / English.

Simon

Il faut partir, Monsieur, sans / dire adieu.

Alceste

Speak to me in English will you
or I'll fucking kill you.

(*He grabs Simon, but after a moment relaxes his grip.
Simon disdainfully disengages himself and continues with
his preparations of the room.*)

I'm sorry. Look I'm sorry I spoke
to you like that.

(*He looks round the room.*)

What is this then? Some kind of practical joke?

(*John appears, laughing softly. He too is dressed in an
elaborate seventeenth-century costume – and all subsequent
entries will be in costumes in the extravagant style of Louis'
court – the men rivalling the women. Only Alceste remains*)

in his original clothes.)

John
What's wrong? Have you forgotten about the party?

Alceste
Party? I was asleep –
or at least I was until that gallic creep
woke me up. You're not really dressing up are you?

John
I already have – and I've got something here for you.

(*He gives Alceste a box.*)

Alceste
What's this?

John
Open it.

Alceste
D'you know I was dreaming
of wild animals. They were screaming
and biting into the most vulnerable places
imaginable. Then I saw they all had human faces.

(*Pause.*)

What is this?

John
A wig.

Alceste
(*faint laugh*)
No. I'm sorry.

83

John

Come on. You're not going to let everybody
down? It would look bad.

Alceste

You must be mad
if you think I'm wearing this.

John

It might be an improvement.

Alceste

Don't take the piss
out of me.

John

I don't honestly see what harm a / wig can –

Alceste

I don't participate in costume fucking drama.

John

Put it on.

Alceste

No.

(*John tries to put the wig on Alceste who resists with
increasing violence.*)

John

Come on. You're so *uptight*.

Alceste

Just take it off. Take it off. I'm not having it. Alright?

(*He throws the wig down. Pause. John picks it up and*

smooths it.)

John

Was that strictly necessary? Wigs are expensive.
Listen, why / can't you –

Alceste

Yes. I know. I'm being childish and offensive
et cetera et cetera. Well let me reimburse
you. Nothing could be worse,
could it, than being in your debt.
Come on. How much? Cash or cheque?

(*He reaches for his money.*)

John

(*embarrassed*)

Please.

Alceste

Everything has a price,
and if my own particular vice
is to express my undying hatred
of human nature, then I'm quite prepared to pay for it.

John

Come *on* …

Alceste

Come on *what*?
'Be reasonable'? That's about the only argument you've
got.
Can you really tell me to my face
that you love the human race?
Or being in this artificial place?
That you don't dream of somewhere out in space

where this shallow world is not 'all that is the case'?

John

No, no. Absolutely fine.
You don't need (obviously) to read Wittgenstein
to know that even by his or her own evaluation
man is an imperfect creation.
OK?
Our world is shallow. Accepted.
It doesn't follow that you have to reject it.
Surely its very superficiality
is what gives rise to interesting strategies
for survival. If there's no intrinsic meaning
then the fun is to invent one. This evening's
party is a perfect example.
How can you possibly perceive it as harmful?
I'm getting depressed by all your crises.
What good are all your so-called virtues if you can't
    enjoy their corresponding vices.

(*Offers the wig again.*)

Come on: do it for me.

Alceste

I've had enough for one day of your Mr Feel-Good
    philosophy.
Strategies? Meaning? Imperfection?
You have a wonderful gift for self-deception.
You claim academic innocence
while providing the rationale for decadence
of every kind. Every corrupt society enlists
its own tame apologists
and you're turning into one of them:
the kind of person
who paints over a moral mess
with borrowed intellectual fancy-dress.

John

(Please, please, please …)

Alceste

Look at you. It's embarrassing.

John

(*shrugs*)

Embarrassing? It's fun.

Alceste

No. I'm sorry. Not everyone
would agree that what went on at Versailles
was 'fun'. Just try
imagining a church and state
monitoring every move you make:
what you write, what you think, who you meet …

John

OK, OK. You're still drunk. Why don't you just go
  back to sleep?

Alceste

I'm quite sober.
And I tell you: when this party's over
I'm going. And I'm taking Jennifer
out of this. I'm just waiting for
the right moment to tell her. In the morning this will
  just seem

John

I know, I know: like a bad dream.
Fine. Well look, I promised I'd meet Ellen at the desk.

(*He heads towards the door.*)

87

Alceste

OK. You know, I'm not depressed
about this. She's going to agree.
I know that secretly she has great respect for me.

John

Absolutely. Well there's no telling
what will happen. I must go down and see Ellen.

(*John goes out.*
A moment passes. We hear voices and laughter. Jennifer and
Covington emerge from the bedroom, both in beautiful cos-
tumes, Jennifer holding Covington's script from Act One. They
are not aware of Alceste concealed in the chair downstage.)

Covington

I wrote the part specifically for you.
You know how much I adore
your work.

Jennifer

Well, thank you.

Covington

      And perhaps if you could use your
influence and show this to a producer ... ?
It's conceived for the stage but could be
very easily developed into a full-scale movie.

(*Pause. He looks at her.*)

Jennifer

What is it?

Covington

(*lowers voice*)

    Alceste. Can I be very personal

and ask if the two of you … ? It's just there are some
  awful
rumours going round and I wondered if there was any
  truth in it.
(By the way: he's not to know you've got this script.)

Jennifer

(*faint laugh*)

Are you hitting on me?
I don't understand. And why the need for secrecy?

Covington

Certain things are best
left unexplained. But it's no secret that I detest
him. (*He takes her hand.*) And the fact is
– yes – I find you extremely extremely attractive.

Alceste

(*reveals himself*)

I'm *sure* you do. And it's obviously mutual
judging from the way you're blushing like a schoolgirl.
You talk about commitment and you let him
into your *bed*room
to what? Discuss his play?
Come on. I wasn't born yesterday.

Covington

Can we please deal with this rationally.
I have no intention of trespassing on your territory.

Alceste

And I have no intention of waiting
here watching you salivating.

Covington

She obviously prefers Neanderthals.

Alceste

No no. She clearly prefers the company of fools.

Covington

(*goes to Jennifer*)

I won't make a scene. He's obviously frightened.

Alceste

You? Make a scene? You can't even *write* one.

Covington

(*to Jennifer*)

I really think you ought to intervene.

Alceste

(*to Jennifer*)

I think it's time you told us what / all this *means*.

Covington

Isn't there some way of / *pacifying* him?

Alceste

Refusing to speak isn't going to satisfy anyone.

Covington

You're not really in love with this paralytic?

Alceste

You're not really sleeping – are you – with a critic?

Jennifer

Boys, boys. It must be time for your medication.
I feel like I'm in an institution watching the patients.
D'you really think I'm such a child
that I can't make up my own mind?
D'you both respect me so little
that resolving your own quarrel
is more important than considering my feelings?
Quite frankly nothing could be less appealing
to me than your undisguised
jealousy. And someone's going to be unpleasantly
  surprised
when they *do* see
the real me.
If you were even remotely sensitive
– either of you – you'd know that I'm being tentative
only because I find you both rather scary.

(to Alceste)

And what's wrong with you? You haven't said a word
  about what I'm wearing.

Covington

Then let me apologize. But even so
you can't equivocate.

Alceste

And I have a *right* to know.
Just what *is* the truth?
What *is* the 'real you'?
The dress,
yes,
is very beautiful ...

Jennifer

Thank you.

Alceste

... but entirely – and stunningly – superficial.
If this ... man really is your lover
then obviously our relationship is over.
I apologize for my previous (yes, I'm sorry) violence
but please see that you no longer have a right to silence.

Covington

Absolutely. Prevaricating
like this is simply self-incriminating.

Jennifer

Oh, is that a fact?
What is this? Some kind of British neo-fascist double-act?
I've told you: you'll both just have to keep waiting.
Ellen! My *God!* You look totally *devastating!*

(*Ellen has appeared in costume, accompanied by John.
Laughing, she kisses cheeks with Jennifer.*)

I'm so pleased to see you. I had visions
of being burned by the inquisition
here. These two charming creatures
are worse than the Society of fucking Jesus.
Thank God I have an ally.
Look at them: can't you see they're just dying
to get the thumbscrews out.

Ellen

(*tries to take her aside*)

Listen, there's something we need to talk about.

Jennifer

(*laughing*)

Seriously. I was scared.

Ellen

(*as before*)

No. Listen. I think you need to be prepared / for this.

Covington

Is there something we're not supposed to hear?

Jennifer

Can't you just fuck off for a moment. Go on. /
Disappear.

Alceste

Don't talk to him like that. You've no right / to be abu-
sive.

Jennifer

No right? Since when did you acquire this interest in
what is or is not polite?
Give me some space, OK? I just want
to speak privately to my … whatever you are.

Ellen

Confidante.

Jennifer

Confidante. Exactly.

(*Before they can speak Julian, Alex and Marcia – all cos-
tumed – enter brusquely carrying bundles of the evening
paper which they dump on the floor.*)

Julian

Well, well, well. They do indeed exist:
the mythical female icon and the uncompromising
journalist.

Alex

(*coldly*)

> Jenny darling, what a wonderful dress.
> And Ellen – let's all drink shall we to the freedom of
> the gutter press.

(*Alex and Simon hand out champagne over the following.*)

Ellen
(I tried to / warn you.)

Marcia
Yes, yes, yes. I know you can't stand the sight of me
but remember darling, you did invite me.
I was just gluing on my beauty spot
when I got
the most amazing phone call from Alex
asking me if I'd seen the evening paper.
                Of course we all know how he panics
– don't you Alex – so of course I read the piece
expecting it to be just sleaze,
the usual nasty prying journalese.
But unless you've been seriously misquoted
then even someone like myself … a devoted
friend … I mean I'm all for speaking one's mind,
but …

Julian
I think you're being far too kind,
Marcia. The whole thing quite frankly stinks.

Alex
I mean if this is really what she thinks / of us …

Julian
I don't know which is more demeaning:

saying it or printing it. Yes, we've all been
hurt sometimes by the papers – but never attacked
like this. Let me read a typical extract:
'It's awesome to be sitting just feet away from a young
   woman whose controversial screen performances
   have divided the critics and become iconic for
   generation X'
blah blah blah
'My first question is about her relationship with
   superbrat –'
thank you very much
'– actor Julian St. John Smith, a frequent visitor to her
   luxury penthouse suite. She is surprisingly frank.'
and I quote:
'Julian is a kind of caricature of all the bad things you
   hear about the English – inbred, class-obsessed, vain
   and emotionally retarded. He's also a terrible actor.'
unquote.

Jennifer
Ellen, this was *not part* of the interview.

Julian
Excuse me. May I continue?
'I ask her what it's like to meet Covington, a critic who
   has consistently championed her work on this side of
   the Atlantic. She gives a sphinx-like smile and says:'
quote
'Menopausal male critics have a tendency to admire
   any young woman who takes her clothes off in front
   of the camera. I'm sure he was thrilled to meet me
   but I can't say that the thrill was mutual.'
unquote.

Jennifer
I don't understand. You've abused our friendship.

Marcia

You should be more careful who you get into bed with.

Alex

(*takes over reading*)

'Over vodka martinis on the roof garden with its stun-
ning panorama of the river the conversation turns to
top actors' agent Alexander Alvi. Is it true, I ask,
that without Alex she'd never have made the transition to major star status? Her response is refreshing-
ly blunt: "Alex's input into my career has been less
than zero. He has his own reasons for cultivating me
– well two reasons to be precise – greed and lust." I
ask / her finally ...'

Jennifer

Alex ...

(*Slight pause.*)

Alex

'I ask her finally to comment on her much-rumoured
relationship with writer Alceste. Is he, I suggest, a
kind of father figure to her? She stares for a while
into her glass before gazing up at me with her cool
blue eyes. "I can't think of anyone," she says, "less
like my father, who is gentle, quiet, respected and
respectful of others. Alceste thinks of himself as a
kind of misanthrope, but I suspect that at heart he's
just another good old-fashioned misogynist."
Her outspoken self-confidence makes it hard to believe
that this beautiful young woman has only just
emerged from her teens ...'
et cetera et cetera.

(*He lets the paper fall.*
Silence.)

Jennifer

I thought we were friends, Ellen. I invited you here as a
    guest.

Ellen

I have my career to think of – and I do believe this is in
    the public interest.

Alex

Well Jenny, you are a real model of loyalty –
what wonderful news for the whole agency.
(We're going to need more than lawyers to handle
this kind of scandal.)

Julian

Great article. *Loved* the style.
No, I really don't think it's worth my while
getting angry. Who cares about you and your dykey
friend when I can have any woman I bloody well like.

Covington

And what about my script?
She promised me she'd commit to it!
She's obviously made so many promises
they've become meaningless.
Well, I've behaved like a complete idiot
haven't I. But at least you've made me realize it
in time. I'm sure you'll always be in the news
Jenny. Just don't expect any more good reviews.

(*to Alceste*)

I apologize for what happened earlier on today.
Obviously I have no intention of standing in your way.

Marcia

I came here as you can imagine fully intending
to take your side – desperately wanting to defend
you – but you are clearly, my darling, morally deformed.
And I have to say to everyone: you *were* warned.
(And how anyone could write this kind of feature
with no reference whatsoever to Jenny's most significant
    teacher ...)
But the person who must be the most cut up
and hurt is this poor man / whose integrity –

Alceste

                                    Just shut up
will you for once. You're not my wife,
and you can kindly keep your nose out of my emotional
    life.
Don't think I don't know the price
you're asking for taking my side in this –
a considerable amount
(and I don't think I could bring myself to settle the
    account).

Marcia

Don't flatter yourself. *Wife?* What makes you think I'd
    want to be
sold into paternalistic slavery
with you? Marriage is just an anachronism
darling – a relic of late twentieth century capitalism
or didn't you know? And I think I'd be afraid to get my
    kicks
from Jennifer's rejects.
(After all I'm not someone who happily caters
for people of dubious immunological status.)
I have no wish to 'come between you' whatsoever
and I'm sure you'll be terribly terribly terribly happy
    together.

Alceste

So. You've all had your little say
then, just like in an old play
where everyone makes a speech.

(*Pause.*)

                              And now it's my turn,
only for once / I ...

Jennifer

                    OK, OK everyone, burn
me then, at the stake. You're after
blood – clearly – and hey! I'm the martyr.
Mistakes have been made – yes –
and I can see that this is where I'm expected to confess
et cetera et cetera and beg forgiveness.
But as God is my witness
I'm no more guilty of deception
than any other person standing in this room –
with perhaps one notable exception.

(*to Alceste*)

You're the only one here who doesn't take me
for granted. And you have every right to hate me.
I'm sorry.

Alceste

                    D'you think I'm so disloyal
as to judge you by a soundbite in a newspaper article?
It's obvious to me you've been provoked
into making these comments. (*to Ellen*) And I'd've
    hoped
that for all your intellectual wheeler-dealing
you might have spared some thought for this girl's
    feelings.
How you can vandalize

99

a person's soul in search of scandal is
beyond me. Fortunately the truth of human
nature can't be condensed into your squalid little
    column.

(*to Jennifer*)

Listen: we have so much in common:
we're quick to be judgemental
and both unfashionably sentimental
and this is what I propose:
no more films, acting, parties, interviews.
Quit the city. Forget work. Turn our backs
on all of this. Begin to relax.
Just the two of us.
We can become anonymous.
We'll buy a little house
with a garden – trees – a stream – whatever.
Then we could think about starting – don't you see – a /
    family together.

Jennifer

(*crescendo of disbelief*)

No, no, no, no, no, no, no … *What*? *Leave*?
What're you trying to *do* to me? This is the air I
    breathe.

Alceste

We don't *need* these people. This hotel,
these costumes – it's like an ante-room to hell.
Look at them, Jennifer. *They* don't care.

Jennifer

(*faint laugh*)

You're seriously asking me to join you in some kind of

    suburban nightmare?
    Shop? Cook? Clean? What? Do the dishes? *Sleep?*
    Drive the kids to ballet in a Japanese *jeep?*

(*Ellen laughs softly.*)

    'These people' are still (I hope) my friends – *and*
    – like it or not – this is the world I understand.

(*She takes Ellen's arm. The others grin, now they see the tide
is turning against Alceste.*)

    Maybe right now they're temporarily
    a little mad at me
    – but I know they'll soon enough forgive me.
    Won't you?

                           Alex

(*smiling*)

                        Jenny …

(*She offers her hand to Alex. He laughs and kisses it.*)

                         Jennifer
                      Don't you see?
    And Julian – he *loves* to be my slave
    really – kicked, whipped and made to behave
    – don't you boy? It's a sado-masochistic need
    entirely characteristic of the breed.

(*Julian lets his tongue hang out and pants rapidly like a dog.
Jennifer laughs and offers her hand. He kisses it languorous-
ly. She strokes his face. Everyone except Alceste laughs.
Without releasing Julian she turns to Alceste.*)

    It might've been fun for us to have an *affair,*
    but I've just turned twenty, and I'm not *going* any-
        where.

(*The others all laugh softly.*)

(*intensely*)

    I love the city – and the night.
    And no way will I abandon them without a fight.
    Simon.

Simon
    Madame?

Jennifer
         He makes such a wonderful
servant and his French is impeccable.
Let's have some music. And nothing too arty.
I'm sick of this. I want to party.

(*The others laugh. Simon begins to play boogie-woogie on the harpsichord, but after a moment Alceste makes a violent gesture – bangs down the lid, or smashes a plaster cupid – and the music stops.*)

Alceste
If that's the life you want to lead,
so be it. Just don't come to me when you need
help, because I shan't be there.
You may not believe in despair
but I do. It's a kind of pit
and you're digging yourself deeper and deeper into it.

(*He walks out. Embarrassed laughter.*)

John
It's so typical of him to overreact.
Don't worry: I'll run and bring him straight back.

(*John moves towards the exit, but at an imperceptible gesture from Jennifer, Simon and Alex block his way.*)

What're you doing? Look: I want to leave.

I'm worried about him.

Ellen

Relax, John, just relax. Don't you see
we're better off without him.